The Zen Teachings of Daiho Hilbert Roshi

Volume 1

*A collection of Daiho Roshi's blog
posts and other writings*

Edited by, and with an introduction by,
Luis KaiUn Lista

Foreword by
Tim Ryuko Langdell, Roshi

Still Center Publications
Oxford/Pasadena 2026

Oxbridge Publishing, Inc.
Still Center Publications
Pasadena, California 91101
www.stillcenterpublications.com
www.stillcenter.org

Library of Congress Cataloging-in-Publication Data
Hilbert, Harvey
    The Zen Teachings of Daiho Hilbert: Volume 1/ Ed. by Luis Lista
    pages cm
      ISBN: 978-1-954971-07-3
      1. Zen Buddhism. I. Hilbert, Harvey, II. Lista, Luis, III. Langdell, Tim

9 8 7 6 5 4 3 2 1

FIRST EDITION

Contents

FOREWORD

A Vietnam war veteran and a Purple Heart recipient, Daiho Roshi is a psychotherapist and an expert on PTSD as well as being the founder of the Order of Clear Mind Zen in Las Cruces, New Mexico. Despite being shot in the head, leading the significant left-side paralysis, Daiho went on to college, earning both a masters and PhD.

Daiho Roshi is the dharma heir (successor) of Ken Hogaku Shozen McGuire Roshi, from whom he received transmission both as a Zen priest and as a Roshi. Roshi roughly translates from Japanese as "venerable teacher," and is often also translated as Zen Master. The term means that a student has received full and complete transmission from their teacher, in is said to have received "inka shomei." A Roshi is given the honor—and with it, the obligation—to sustain and build the specific Zen lineage. In this instance, the lineage is that of Soyu Matsuoka Roshi, the Japanese Zen Master who gave transmission to Shozen McGuire Roshi, and who was one of the first Soto Zen Masters to bring Zen to the west in the late 1930s. I, too, am in this lineage, having been given inka shomei by Daiho Roshi as a Roshi in the Matsuoka lineage.

At the time of writing, we are still clarifying the details of Matsuoka Roshi's life, however it seems Dr. Soyu Matsuoka (1912-1997) was born near Hiroshima. He attended Soto-shu's Komazawa University in Tokyo where he earned a bachelor's degree and then gained a PhD in philosophy from Political Science University in Tokyo. He then goes on to complete his training as a Soto Zen Priest at Soji-ji, one of the two main Soto-shu monasteries along with Eihei-ji. Around the year 1243, Dogen Zenji, the Japanese founder of Soto Zen, inherited a temple known as Daibutsu-ji which he renamed as Eihei-ji in 1246. Naturally, Eihei-ji became one of the head temples for the Japanese Soto sect—

known as Soto-shu. Keizan Jokin (1268-1325) is considered the second great founder of Soto-shu in Japan, and he founded the temple Soji-ji, the second head Soto temple, where Matsuoka was trained.

Matsuoka is given an early task while resident at Soji-ji of establishing a Soto temple in the far north of Japan on remote island named Karafuto. From all accounts, despite the near impossibility of his assignment, Matsuoka was successful in this task although unfortunately whatever he established was likely destroyed when Russia claimed the island in about 1945. We believe that it was Matsuoka's success, though, in establishing the temple on Karafuto that led to Soto-shu assigning him to be one of the earliest emissaries to the U.S. to support the Japanese population in America. In or about 1938 or 1939 (we have two conflicting reports), Matsuoka is recorded as arriving by boat in Los Angeles where he was assigned to Zenshu-ji, one of the few established Soto temples in the U.S. Then after some time in Los Angeles at Zenshu-ji, Matsuoka is recorded as being assigned to supervisor Sojo-ji in San Francisco, the Soto-shu temple that Shunryu Suzuki would later be assigned to in 1959.

This places Matsuoka in America many years before the arrival of better-known early Soto Zen Masters who brought Zen to the west such as Shunryu Suzuki (Zen Center of San Francisco) who arrived in 1959 and Taizan Maezumi (Zen Center of Los Angeles) who arrived in 1956. However, by as early as 1943 we have records of Matsuoka applying for permission to establish a "Buddhist Church" in Chicago at 693 Marshfield Avenue, which becomes Matsuoka's first U.S. Zen temple. Interestingly, though, even in 1943, the authorities show Matsuoka has a recorded permanent residence address in Pasadena, California rather than in Chicago.

According to word-of-mouth records, Matsuoka spent a brief period in Japanese internment camps, where he taught zazen to those interned there. However, it appears to have been a short-lived internment, with Matsuoka's fluency in English being seen as a benefit to American military understanding Japanese. He is released on condition that he remain in the Chicago area. After the war, Matsuoka established the Zen Buddhist Temple of Chicago (also apparently known as Chicago Zenshu Bukkyokai) which still exists to this day. It is during this period that Matsuoka switches from his assigned role as a Soto Zen priest tasked with supporting primarily Japanese Americans, to focusing on teaching American students. He splits from Soto-shu, only presenting his first one or two novice priests to Soto-shu in Japan, and then becomes independent of Japan as an emergent new *American* Zen tradition. Then in the early 1950s Matsuoka is said to have gone to New York to study under D.T. Suzuki at Columbia, which studies further established Matsuoka as someone bringing Zen to a western audience. The range of locations Matsuoka teaches in the 1950s and onwards shows his new direction, teaching police associations, karate schools, the YMCA and even became a special instructor at Colorado State University.

Shozen McGuire studied with Matsuoka starting in around 1963 and later moved to New Mexico where he founded Daibutsu-ji temple. McGuire takes Shukke Tokudo (priest ordination) from Matsuoka in 1968 and is then given full dharma transmission (inka shomei) in 1977. Later, Daiho Hilbert studies with McGuire Roshi at Daibutsu-ji and is first given priest ordination by McGuire, and then inka shomei. At this point, Daiho Roshi leaves Daibutsu-ji to establish the Order of Clear Mind Zen, a socially engaged sangha (community) in Las Cruces, New Mexico.

This first volume of Daiho Roshi's teachings is part of a concerted effort by Still Center Publications to publish not only the teachings of Matsuoka, but also those of his dharma heirs, notable among which is Daiho Roshi. As you will see, Daiho's teaching style has similarities to that of Matsuoka who split from the more traditional style of Soto-shu in favor of an everyday Zen style tailored for an American audience.

Dr. Tim Ryuko Langdell, Roshi
Still Center Zen, Pasadena, California. February 2026.

Daiho Hilbert Roshi

INTRODUCTION

It is with deep gratitude and great respect that we present this first volume of the teachings of Harvey So Daiho Hilbert Roshi, given between 2005 and 2006.

These precious teachings bear witness to the living transmission of the Dharma within the Sōtō Zen lineage, a tradition that traces back to the great masters Dōgen Zenji and Keizan Zenji and continues to flourish today through devoted teachers such as Hilbert Roshi.

Sōtō Zen emphasizes the practice of zazen, silent seated meditation, as the direct path to realizing our true nature. Rather than seeking a spectacular awakening or intellectualizing the truth, the practice of Sōtō Zen invites us to simply "sit and be," to remain fully present in each moment with great simplicity and profound surrender.

Through these teachings, Hilbert Roshi shares wisdom deeply rooted in an authentic Zen practice, yet also nourished by a keen awareness of the challenges of daily life. His words resonate as an invitation to each of us: to return again and again to the simplicity of posture, to the breath, and to the silent light of our true nature.

As you turn these pages, you will discover not only the precious instructions of an accomplished master but also the spirit of a living transmission that goes beyond words. Daiho Hilbert Roshi does not teach solely through discourse, but through presence, practice, and the example of a life dedicated to the Dharma. Every word recorded here carries the mark of this authenticity, this commitment to the Buddha's path, and the simplicity of its practice, deeply rooted in his daily life and his community.

This volume is not a dogmatic manual but an invitation to direct practice. Zen is not an idea to be understood but a reality to be fully lived. Hilbert Roshi constantly reminds us that the truth of Zen is already present in our breath, our posture, and every aspect of our daily existence. He encourages us to return always to zazen—not to escape the world, but to embrace life as it is, with its joys and difficulties.

This spirit of returning to the essential follows in the footsteps of the lineage transmitted by Soyu Matsuoka Roshi. Trained in Japan before coming to teach in the United States, Matsuoka Roshi had an approach that was both traditional and profoundly pragmatic. He saw Zen as a direct response to modern suffering, a means of restoring inner balance in a world of constant change. It can be said without hesitation that Matsuoka Roshi was a pioneer of Zen in America. Although discreet and focused on daily practice and weekly teachings to his Western disciples, he undoubtedly played a crucial role in introducing Sōtō Zen to the West. His direct and pragmatic approach, deeply rooted in tradition yet open to contemporary realities, shaped an entire generation of practitioners, among whom Hilbert Roshi was an exemplary heir.

Harvey So Daiho Hilbert Roshi inherited this approach and enriched it with his own experience, making it accessible to a growing community of practitioners.

Within this lineage of transmission, it is also important to pay tribute to Tim Ryuko Langdell Roshi, a disciple of Hilbert Roshi, who, like other heirs of Daiho Roshi, continues this work of sharing the Dharma with great devotion and leads the editorial work of this collection of teachings. The transmission of Zen is, above all, a heart-to-heart transmission, from person to person, and each generation brings its unique contribution to this uninterrupted chain.

Please note that this volume strives to respect as faithfully as possible the way So Daiho Roshi originally delivered these teachings. The original titles have been preserved, and the chronological order in which he shared them across various social media platforms (mainly his blogs and websites) has been carefully maintained. Through this, we hope to allow readers to follow the evolution and adaptation of the master's teachings in response to an ever-changing world.

In total, over twenty years of practice and teachings will be compiled in future volumes of Harvey So Daiho Hilbert Roshi's teachings, of which this present work constitutes only the first volume. It is, therefore, an open window into a life of Dharma. His best and worst moments, his loves and heartbreaks, his deep connections with mystical Judaism, his hopes for his disciples and Sangha, as well as his disappointments. Everything is here—without filter or hagiography. These are direct and profound teachings that challenge our relationship to practice, to others, and to the world.

May the reading of these teachings inspire you to deepen your practice, to sit fully in the clarity of the moment, and to allow the Dharma to reveal itself naturally in every aspect of your life. As Hilbert Roshi often reminds us, "Everything you need is already here. Sit, breathe, and simply be present."

May this volume be an offering to the Sangha, a bridge between generations, and a guiding light for practitioners on the timeless path of Zen.

Luis KaiUn Lista
Dharma Winds Zen Sangha/Still Center Zen Europe, Belgium.

1

On Not Chopping Wood Today

Saturday, February 19, 2005

Every morning after zazen I step outside and split wood with my maul. It weighs eight pounds and I am used to the feel of this piece of metal as it splits the twisted rounds of cedar we use to cook with and to heat our Refuge deep in the mountains of southern New Mexico.

I am a Zen Buddhist monk. A married priest in the Soto tradition, who has just split away from his home Temple to create his own. Today, however, I am on the road, in a city where there is no wood to chop. My hands are empty.

So, instead, I sit at a friend's computer and create this blog.

I wonder about the nature of this empty hand. Idle, I am suffering. People who live in this world of convenience, who live without moving their bodies much, do they have a sense of the deep and intimate connection of body and mind that hard, concentrated work provides?

I am reminded of the story of an old Zen monk who failed to eat one day. He is ill and did not work. Alarmed, his brother monks asked that he eat. He said, "No work, no food." Simple elegance.

2

Practice

Tuesday, April 19, 2005

Practice is just something we do every day. It is really nothing special, but then, nothing is. Ours is to just be as simply as we can be.

We may not sit down on a cushion and practice zazen, but as long as we live in each moment with our eyes open and our hearts in the right place, we are practicing Zen.

I try to encourage my students to sit daily, twice daily actually, but I am not always successful. I may not be a very good Teacher.

Still, I sit each night and most every morning. I sit alone usually in my small mountain zendo. It is often cold as the fire in the pot bellied stove has usually gone out. I light incense and a candle. The flame and smoke blanket the brass statue of the Buddha that sits before me. My cushion supports my practice. The light washes my heart. It is quiet and my mind settles finally.

Tomorrow will take care of itself.

3

Rohatsu

Monday, December 12, 2005

This morning is the 8th day of the twelfth lunar cycle of the year: Rohatsu. On this morning the Buddha looked up at the morning star and had a profound realization. He clearly saw that all things in all times are one, of one substance, interdependent and infinite, eternal, and always changing. But then he stood up and took a long walk.

He didn't go anywhere. There is nowhere to go. He was simply present, fully present with whoever he was with and in each moment, there was no difference between he and they. He saw clearly.

We know from his example and from the multitude of buddhas, before and after, that this kind of present moment living is possible even today. With practice and right understanding each of us are buddhas. Some of us are buddhas-in-waiting, but all of us are already buddhas.

As we take our next step into the new year please avoid making big plans. Have a place and live within it as fully as you possibly can: seeing clearly, tasting clearly, smelling clearly, feeling clearly, perceiving and thinking clearly everything just as it is with nothing added. This is our way.

On my calendar this morning it says:

Bring me a pearl from the bottom of the sea without getting wet.

What does this mean? If you read the words and get stuck in them you do not understand. What pearl? What sea? What does it mean "to bring"? What is "getting wet?"

When we understand this is not about thinking, not about words, but rather about correct action, then we are on the path. Our lives become actual expressions of that path.

What is your expression?

4

Correct Thinking

Monday, December 12, 2005

We are preparing to leave the refuge for the winter months. We have leased an apartment in Las Cruces and will be moving there next weekend. This comes as a sort of acknowledgement, I suppose, that we are not interested in dealing with the harshness of the mountain winter this year. There is a freedom that comes with this decision.

I would like to talk with you a little about this freedom.

Our thinking, as I have suggested to you before, often gets in our way. We all too often over-think things, stumbling this way and that, in our effort to get things right. And sometimes the thinking gives rise to great fear, greed, or hatred: the poisons that paralyze us or push us to do and say that which we would not otherwise do.

In the Zen tradition, we try to think in terms of "right" or "correct" thinking, action, speech, and so on.

Correct thinking is that which allows us to do what the situation calls for. To have correct thinking, we must "see" as clearly as the moon reflected on a still pond's water. When we have a clear mind, it reflects exactly (and only) what is there in front of us, with nothing added. We then know what to do. We call this correct understanding.

Incorrect thinking is that which gets in the way, distorts, poisons, or otherwise disturbs us. It gets in our way and often causes us to wobble along, uncertain of what step to take next or in what direction to take it.

With correct thinking, when we are sick, we see a doctor. We take our medicine. This includes all forms of sickness: physical, psychological, spiritual, and emotional. When depression comes over us, we see a doctor. We take our medicine. When we feel alone and without connection to the heart of the universe, we go to our Three Treasures, the Buddha's example, the Buddha's Teaching and our Friends. We take the Buddha's medicine, stilling our mind, refreshing our heart, and centering ourselves.

Likewise, with correct thinking when the dog barks, we naturally let him out or feed him or otherwise tend to him. If our children break something, fail to acknowledge us, or in some other way 'bother' us, we pick up the pieces, accept them, forgive them, love them, and easily go to the next thing before us to do.

Complaining is "something added."

Complaining, as I so often do, can be a way of letting out the steam we are building in our heads with incorrect thinking. Sometimes it is good to let out the steam. Sometimes not. If others are present, silence is better. Better still is not having the steam arise in the first place. That is our practice. That is our work to be done each day.

When we live this way we are living completely free. Just there. It is in this that we can see that the true shackles are those we create in our minds.

5

Executions

Monday, December 12, 2005

A week or so ago, a Vietnam vet was executed. I think he was the 1000Th person killed by the state since the Supreme Court lifted the ban on capital punishment. Tonight another vet will be killed, though he is a different sort of vet. He is a veteran of the streets. A killer, gangster, no doubt. Perhaps reformed, I don't know.

War does funny things to people. Hell, life does funny things to people. We pride ourselves in our ability to understand our world, learn from our mistakes, grow as a culture, and yet, here we are, living out vengeance.

These executions should cause us to at least take a breath and pause for a moment.

What are we doing?

Retaliation, it seems to me, is a mark of a primitive mind. It is criminal behavior. It is what we expect of gangs and barbarians.

An eye for an eye, people say. Really? When was the last time the state blinded a person or knocked out his tooth? Jews made it nearly impossible to execute someone when convicted. But this "Judeo-Christian" society? Gosh, we have had a thousand opportunities to show mercy and in each case turned away.

We need to keep society safe. Right. And killing people does that? Are we really keeping society safe? Who does the death penalty punish? The one executed or the executioner? Is there a difference? Who really could cast the proverbial first stone? What is the moral foundation of this ethic?

My sense is that we diminish ourselves greatly through state sanctioned killing. But then we are not really a civilized society, are we? We pretend. We talk the talk but abhor the walk. We like to look civilized. But appearances are truly deceiving.

Civilized societies take care of their ill, their elderly, and their poor. Civilized societies do not execute children. Civilized societies do not poison the atmosphere for the sake of a few dollars more to add to the already excessive profits of oil companies. Civilized societies do not sanction the possession of handguns, nor do they need them. Civilized societies provide funding for research to cure lethal illnesses, regardless of who is ill or how they became ill. Civilized societies teach their children and each other how to love. Civilized societies cherish peace, life, and liberty.

We can do better than this. We must.

As we are all one, including the executioner and the executed, I ask we each recite the prayer of atonement for ourselves this evening.

6

In the center

Wednesday, December 21, 2005

In the Center
Sitting quietly
in the center,
the universe all around:
no center, no universe.

7

Sit on your butt ... Not!

Wednesday, December 21, 2005

Our Zen is not a sit on your butt and do nothing Zen. When we sit on our butt we are doing something; we are being Buddha-nature. When we stand. we are doing something, we are standing buddhas. When we are walking, we are walking buddhas. When working we are working buddhas. So our Zen is a Zen in motion. Our Zen is a pure form of being in this world, not separate from it. Our Zen is Buddha himself.

No wobbling allowed. We exist in the world. We see something. We do something.

To do without thinking requires a clear mind that sees clearly what is there. It requires a complete union with buddha-nature, there is this, there is that. They are the same. An I-Thou of the infinite.

Compassion comes naturally to those who live in the world. When we live outside of the world, compassion is much more challenging. Living in the world, we see, feel, taste, smell, the suffering of others. We suffer with them as we are with them. Living outside the world, in our thoughts and feelings and assumptions, it is easy to make judgments about others, others' actions, in-actions, values, attitudes, etc. We see them and ourselves as different, somehow separate from ourselves.

Our practice must take us into the world, deeply into the world, where we exist in the same space as all beings. When we exist in the same space, where is there room for difference? Where is there room for judgment? So, when we exist in the same space we exist in the clear world of nothing added.

8

The Clear World

Friday, December 23, 2005

In the clear world of nothing added, I taste sugar. I taste salt. I taste hot. I taste cold. I do not taste the words. The words are something added. So, when these things come to my tongue and are just there. I am in the clear world of nothing added. I am experience without the "I am." If I say, " I like sweet!" Or "how awful, soooo sour!" I am in the world of something added, and no longer in the experience.

It is our practice to stay as much as possible in one world and not the other. Our world is the world of the direct and present. The other is the world of expectation, valuation, discrimination. One is non-dualistic where everything is one. The other has an "I" separating ourselves from our experience.

At the same time it is also very important to recognize and understand that both worlds are one and there is no two. The world of nothing added is pure, direct, "thus." The world of something added is the world of valuation. Big mind, small mind: Emptiness and form, form and emptiness. Like our breath, these things open and close, rise and fall in a rhythm all their own.

Our practice is to join this rhythm. Feel this rhythm. Accept this rhythm.

This is a serious practice, the practice of living in the clear world of nothing added. It is difficult because the mind is a tricky, very quick, little rascal. It is untrained and unwilling to be trained. It resists training. It runs from training! It shouts. It cries. It demands. It's a two-year-old baby having a tantrum. It wants to have a purpose: and its purpose is to think.

Training our minds to live in both worlds as one without hindrance is our practice, and it is very simple. It is just to taste the sweet. Just to taste the sour. It is also to recognize a thought is just a thought, and a feeling is just a feeling. How hard is that?

Open your mouth and taste. Open your eyes and see.

9

Just Be

Saturday, December 24, 2005

The recent comments regarding reducing violence have been floating around my mind over the last several days. This is neither good nor bad. When we have something on our minds, in one sense, it means that we are paying attention to something. Yet, in another sense means we are being distracted by thought and, therefore, not seeing clearly.

Thinking about reducing violence and being peace will not make it happen, just as thinking about enlightenment will not bring it to your mind.

Practice realization, as Master Dogen points out, is just practice. One thing already containing the other, but (in a very special sense) in motion. There is no thinking about peace. There is just peace. There is no thinking about reducing or eliminating violence, there is just being the elimination of violence, period.

We accomplish this through being these things.

Just as in any other aspect of our practice, right understanding provides a clear framework for all that follows. Clear mind is right understanding. From clear mind comes right thought, speech, action, livelihood, effort, mindfulness, and meditation.

To be "right" means to be from the center: direct expressions of buddha-nature. This is non-equivocating compassion.

So, when we set out to bring about peace, we are already mistaken. Just as polishing a tile will not make a mirror. Just as sitting zazen will not make a buddha. We are buddha from the beginning. Do not set out. Just be.

10

Routine

Monday, December 26, 2005

This morning as I opened my eyes the desert sun was rather high. I vowed to see with clear eyes and reduce violence, then got out of bed to make the coffee, walk the dogs --- who were very patient --- and begin my day.

There is something very beautiful about routine. Routines, everyday rituals, are the hangers and organizers of our everyday. In one sense they make everyday events special. In another sense we recognize their everydayness.

When we are young we want to press against the everyday, breaking it, no, smashing it, on the ground of change. Our goal is to experience our limits and push them. Not bad. We expand our minds and bodies. We grow stretching toward the light of day.

As we age, we shift our gears little by little, wanting to have a break. We begin to view change as a threat sometimes or at the least an inconvenience. We begin to delight in the common. We take comfort in the sameness of daily routine.

As we age more, we look back. Sometimes wanting not to let go of that youthful vigor and excitement we once were possessed by. At other times we welcome this opportunity to review. Review deepens our understanding. It contextualizes the processes of life. Blessed perspective.

In each of these times, our orientation is seemingly different. Zen teaches us that they are the same, however, and it is our effort to grip something tightly that is problematic and in the processes disallows us the moment and all that it has to offer us.

When we rise, at whatever age, and vow to see things clearly, that is enough. For then we are seeing without lusting, seeing for seeing itself. It is in this moment that we are truly free.

Practice.

11

City Life

Wednesday, December 28, 2005

It is a sunny morning here in the desert southwest. Morning zazen is done. A breakfast of noodle kugel and sour cream is done. The dogs have been out. Shortly we will walk over to the gym and lift weights, run, and walk on the treadmill. Then it will be time to return some things, eat lunch, pick up some groceries and come home.

Life in the city is so much different from life at the Refuge.

Last night we had guests for dinner. The night before we had guests for dinner. We rarely had guests at the Refuge: too difficult to access.

At the Refuge we planned our trips to the store as a trip to the store was a trip to town and was a trip of six hours or more. Here in the city there are many jewels to attract the eye of desire: books, household things, people. At the Refuge, the jewels were just there, like a breath: the trees, the sun, the animals, the silence.

It is rather like living in Big Mind and Little Mind. We must see them as essentially the same. Navigating freely without trepidation, we center ourselves through our practice of zazen and through the practice of daily ritual. Things here, people there, vast emptiness everywhere. When we are non-attached, non-invested, and are willing to embrace life on its own terms, then we are free.

Non-attachment does not mean non-caring. Non-attachment does not mean a lack of choice and discernment. Values are buddha-nature, they arise through our actions. Non-attachment means acceptance that this is and that is. We engage to assist when assistance is required. We engage to love. We engage to nurture. We disengage to love. We disengage to nurture. All part of the natural processes of life itself.

12

Clear Mind Zen

Friday, December 30, 2005

Today I met with the priests that comprise most of the Board of Daibutsuji. We discussed many things, schedules, sangha needs, etc. But most importantly, we agreed to establish our own school of Zen Buddhism in America, severing our links to Sotoshu in Japan.

Our school will be called "Clear Mind" and our focus will be on the development of Zen as an everyday practice. Our hope is to redefine religion from its western sense of worship of a deity to a sacralization of daily life.

We will practice from a Soto tradition but not be limited to it.

Zen in America must become a uniquely American experience and practice. To do so means we must leave Japan to the Japanese and walk our own path.

13

Authenticity

Sunday, January 1, 2006

Zen is neither Japanese or American, Chinese or German, Zen is just Zen. We should leave all such distinctions aside. We are about practice. We practice to discover our true nature. We practice to be buddhas.

When we come to Zen, however, a Teacher and his or her Zen Center practices with a set of clothes, a language, and a set of customs, if you will. It is these clothes, languages, and the assumptions that go with them that create "American Zen" or Japanese Zen" or some other "Zen."

When I say we are severing our ties with Soto Shu, I mean that we are setting out on our own, walking in our own authority, and not being tied emotionally, financially, or in any other way, to Soto.

My Teacher's Teacher (my dharma grandfather) Matsuoka-roshi was a Soto Zen Bishop. He was sent to America to establish Zen Centers and bring the dharma here to the US. He was assigned here by Sojiji, a training center in Japan. He was a poor monk, not clever or sophisticated with money. While he managed to establish several Zen Centers on both coasts, he took very little money and had little to share with Sojiji. Now Japanese Zen is all about authority, control, and money. If Matsuoka sent the money everything was fine. When Matsuoka could not send the money, things were not fine.

Our model here in the US is his. We make little money from the dharma, ceremonies, ordinations. We modify our ceremonies to fit our neighborhoods and the cultures we exist in. This is classic Zen Buddhism. Adapting, changing, growing: a dynamic, living, force. Soto training centers such as Sojiji seem to be bent on continuing their existence for the purpose of regulating and authenticating (for a fee, of course) Zen.

Humbug.

Want to know Zen? Sit on a cushion and face a wall. With practice comes clear mind, with clear mind comes clear thinking and all of the other paths of our way.

So here we are in a New Year. Let us rejoice in our own authority!

14

Morning Coffee

Tuesday, January 3, 2006

I pour the coffee.
I cannot pour the coffee.
I just pour the coffee.

Depending on your understanding, each statement makes sense or doesn't make sense.

We should not mistake our words for true nature. Words are just thoughts as sound. We live with words. They assist us to communicate. Yet they often distort or destroy our communication. Coffee is not coffee. Pouring is not pouring. Yet coffee is coffee and pouring is pouring.

Our practice assists us in not mistaking coffee for coffee. Our practice helps us see coffee as coffee.

Clear Mind Zen. Soto Zen. Rinzai Zen. Korean Zen. Vietnamese Zen. Chinese Zen. Words. All the same or different?

If you say they are the same you are mistaken. If you say they are different, you are mistaken.

Just pour the coffee.

15

Cleaning the Zendo

Sunday, January 8, 2006

Yesterday's Zazenkai was a good practice. We sat three periods in the morning, walked a half mile to have lunch, returned, sat again two periods, cleaned the Zen Center, sat again two periods and went home.

There was nothing special about this day. The opportunity to mindfully refill the lamps, dust the butsudan, sweep the floors, was ordinary. Sitting on the cushion was ordinary. Bowing was ordinary. Lighting incense was ordinary. Chanting the Heart Sutra was ordinary. Reciting the Four Great Vows was ordinary.

We just did these things, as they came time to be done. When we go through a day like this we are buddhas.

16

Ten Ox-Herding Pictures

Stage One and Two

Monday, January 9, 2006

Anu, a friend from Africa, recently asked us to discuss the Ten Ox-Herding Pictures on our Zen Living Yahoo Group. I am posting each stage and my response here in my blog.

Anu writes: *It appears that all that is known about the author of the verses to the ten ox-herding pictures, master Kakuan Shion, is that he was a disciple of Daizui Genjo [1065-1135] and the twelfth in the line of master Rinzai. His dates of birth and death as well as other information are unclear.*

Stage 1: Seeking the Ox

Seeking the ox incessantly you brush aside thick grasses in pursuit;

The waters are wide, the mountains far, and the path leads on without end. Sapped of strength, exhausted in spirits, knowing no longer where to search,

You only hear the sound of the evening cicadas chirping in the maple trees.

So Daiho:

May 29th, 1966. The Central Highlands of Vietnam, near the Cambodian border. It is night. Very dark. The jungle is quite wet. I have just been in a fire fight with a whole lot of North Vietnamese soldiers. They have us surrounded.

I feel my head. There is a hole in it. I am terrified. Gunfire and grenades build this fear.

I hear the screaming of the dead and dying. I am tired but cannot go to sleep. I fear I might not wake up. I look to the sky, what I can see of it through the dark canopy of trees. It is a black hole in the universe. I ask G-d to save me.

No answer.

In the morning the few of us who survived being overrun are med evacuated out. I leave Vietnam unable to use the left side of my body. I am 19 and a high school dropout with a GED.

What's my next step?

Stage Two:

Anu writes:

He has understood the meaning of the sutras and knows about the tracks through the teachings. It is clear to him that all vessels are made of gold, and he knows that the myriad things are himself. But if he cannot distinguish between right and wrong, how can he separate the true from the false? As he has not yet entered this gate, he can be said to have merely seen the tracks. Btw, background to the introduction . . .To each of the ten pictures of the Ten Ox-

herding Pictures Master Kakuan has first put a "Verse", and at the end his disciple, Jion (some say Kakuan himself, others say the friend of Kakuan) is said to have put a "General Introduction" to the entire work as well as a "Brief Introduction" to each one of the Verses.

Stage 2 : Finding the Tracks

At the waters edge, under the trees - hoofmarks are numerous.
Balmy grasses grow abundantly - can you see them or not?
Even if you go deeper and deeper into the mountains,
How could his nostrils, well compassing the heavens, hide him at all?

So Daiho:

So, at 19 on the streets of Miami with a "Retirement" certificate from the US Army and a body that only half worked, I set out to discover life. Here's the thing: trauma disrupts cognitive and emotional processes. Those of us who have experienced such things, 'know the sutras' but are suddenly on their outside looking in. There is a crack in that cosmic egg that has nurtured us and kept us asleep for so long and now the brilliant light of day is streaming down and we squeeze our eyes, not knowing which way to turn.

I attend peace rallies. I attend college. I sleep with women. I drink. I ride a motorcycle. I read books. I learn to play chess at a chess club. I find jobs and lose jobs. The tracks are everywhere. I have found myself in a world without G-d. A world rushing faster and faster and I am on the outside looking in. Do I really want to go there?

17

Ten Ox-Herding Pictures

Stage Three

Tuesday, January 10, 2006

Introduction

> If you attain by way of sounds,
> you will encounter the source of all seeing.
> The six sense organs are each no different from this;
> in all actions, the head is revealed.
> It is like the salty taste of the water,
> the binder in the paint.
> Raise your eyebrows,
> and this is nothing other than THAT itself.

Verse

> The bush warbler sings on the branch.
> The sun is warm, the breeze gentle,
> and the willows on the riverbank are green.
> There is no place you can escape from him.
> That majestic head and horns could never be painted in a picture.

So Daiho:

In all of the women, books and chess, there was still something missing yet demanding to be found. I often found myself sitting on one of the keys waiting for the sun to come up. Fascinated with morning light. Angry. Hurt. Wanting to blame G-d, men, and country.

Such wounds as the wounds of war are forever open.

The sea was rolling in and out. The jobs came and went. So did the wives. Is this all there is?

No. A shadow.

I met a man named Bernie Schmidt. He was a loud man. He was a strong man. He taught me a few things. He taught me about shouting and learning and studying and not taking second best. He taught me compassion did not mean making excuses. He taught me to love without so much concern for white bread notions of normal. He made "joyful noises unto the lord!" But was not a religious man. He offered me a copy of Walden and a copy of The Way of Zen.

Not too long ago my friend of nearly forty years died.

The shadow stirs.

18

Ten Ox-Herding Pictures

Stage Four

Wednesday, January 11, 2006

Introduction

For a long time he has been living in obscurity in the countryside;
today you have met him.
Because he enjoys his former situation so much, it is difficult to drive him out.
He cannot stop loving the fragrant grasses;
his stubborn will is still strong and a wild spirit remains.
If you wish to make him pure and obedient, you must apply the whip.

Verse

You have exhausted all your faculties to take hold of him.
Because his spirit is strong and his strength abundant,
it is difficult to rid him of his habits.
Sometimes he goes to the top of the high plain.

Other times he resides in clouds and smoke.

So Daiho:

Orgasm is like that, so is riding a motorcycle at 90 mph without the headlights at midnight.

We sit in silence and in a moment everything is nothing.
Our eyes flicker.
Pulses are just pulses.

Impulse and impatience are the great teachers subverting themselves.
In the end, we must grab them by their short hairs and speak.
Enough!

19

Smiling

Thursday, January 12, 2006

Smiling is very good practice. Even when we are sad, we should make an effort to smile. Our world has enough pain and suffering, frowns and crying faces. Our practice is to add joy to the universe, and we do this with a simple smile.

Each day, practice smiling. Each day behave as if you are a smiling buddha. In reality, you are, regardless of how you feel that day. When you take on the smile, the universe smiles with you, even if it is in a lot of pain.

The dog barks: smile. The postman brings a bill, and you have little money: smile. Someone treats you with disrespect: smile.

Such practice displaces bad feelings. New, good feeling then has an opportunity to grow. Pie in the sky, you say? Hmmm. I like pie.

20

Practice

Friday, January 13, 2006

There is a cold front moving through the desert. Yet the sun warms the air quickly. Just so, sitting facing the wall.

Zazen is a burning practice. It melts away the self. And as it does, all things become cool springs, welcomed, often devoured as they arise.

We simply eat.

To sit Zazen on a regular basis is to strengthen our effort. It is a practice of the Excellences and the Eightfold Noble Path all rolled into one cucumber sitting upright on a bed of lettuce.

We simply eat.

Soon it is time to rise. Just as when we fill our bellies at the table, we should rise slowly. We should continue holding our mind in ever-present stillness, a sort of stillness in motion, that takes us through our day, concluding once again on the great cushion.

Please enjoy the warmth and the practice it yields.

21

Ten Ox-Herding Pictures

Stage Five

Friday, January 13, 2006

Introduction

Once thoughts rise up even slightly,
they are followed by other thoughts.
Through enlightenment, they become true;
in delusion, they become false.
It is not due to our surroundings that they are there;
they are only produced by our mind.
We must pull the Ox firmly by his tether and
not allow any doubts to enter.

Verse

Whipping does not depart from the body at any moment.
Lest he follow his own whim, entering the dust and dirt.
If you devotedly tame him, he will be pure and gentle.
Without bridle and chains, he will follow you of his own accord.

So Daiho:

I learn unevenly: trying to learn to walk again, I often stumble. Learning to be a therapist, I sometimes fail to listen. Learning to be a human being once again and not a hunter of human beings, I sometimes see myself kill.

Images are the worst: coffee spoons, cigarettes, motorcycles, medals, beads, long hair, beard, no beard, shaved head; badges of this and that. Like mud they stick to my boots and cause me to grunt while walking. I just want to fly. Zazen releases the weight of the badges. Then,

Nice guy. Feminist. Buddha. Vietnam Vet.

Illusions, not even as real as spooks in the night sky.

Faith in our practice is foundational. Coming to the mountain Zendo, meeting my Master, I sit each day. His life is nothing to write home about. Most Masters live this way. Ordinary living that is all. So I don't write home.

It is important to recognize the chimeric quality of thoughts and feelings. As one old friend used to say, "a bag of shells, Harvey, a bag of shells." When we see our thoughts as important or profound or valuable we are lost. When we see them coming and celebrate them we are lost. Only when they are seen for their true nature, the nature of wind across the desert, are they in their proper context.

So here it is: just sit. Sit in the morning. Sit in the evening. And in between, steer yourself directly.

22

In the middle of normal

Friday, January 13, 2006

In the middle of normal, today:
Zazen, breakfast, banking,
grocery shopping, laundry,
house cleaning,
writing and emailing.
The laundry is folded,
hung, and otherwise
put away.
The groceries
are put away.
And our Shabbos dinner
is being prepared.
I have incense lit
in the Zendo
with the door open
so that the fragrance
of sandalwood
moves through the rooms.
Countless smiles:
Life is stillness in motion.

23

Ten Ox-Herding Pictures

Stage Six

Saturday, January 14, 2006

Introduction

The battle is already over, gain and loss are also empty.
He sings a woodcutter's rustic song and whistles a child's tune.
Straddled on the Ox's back, he gazes at the clouds.
Though you call him he will not return;
though you try to catch and hold him, he will not stay.

Verse

>   You mount the ox and want to make your way slowly home.
>   A barbarian plays the flute in the red glow of sunset.
>   Each measure, each tune is filled with ineffable tones.
>   Among true intimates, what need is there for words?

So Daiho:

Mind comes and goes like the clouds in the sky, as do all things, when we attain oneness with them all, in whatever form, we are on the Ox. We are pure joy. We have attained the realm of emptiness and see ourselves as having arrived. All things are meaningless. All things are fleeting. Since we cannot keep anything, there is no need to value anything. Then 'among true intimates, what need is there for words?' The sea talks to itself in deep silence.

Still, we have not attained the deep abiding. We see bliss as something separate from pain. When the sea is the sea that is not all there is: waves are there also.

A magician flips the coin and in the sound of the spin we are two.

We see good as something different from evil. Vietnam. Killing. Wal-Mart. Shopping. Eating. Shitting. Hugging. Loving. Not different, yet different. We do not understand the coin.

24

Seiza

Saturday, January 14, 2006

Sitting seiza our hands held in gentle repose; the heart and body settles as we open to the universe. Seiza is a traditional kneeling position. Often used by women and used in Tea Ceremony, it possesses great elegance on the one hand, and positions the body in a receptive form, allowing a gentle face to emerge, on the other.

To sit seiza, simply kneel. Place your hands in the Cosmic mudra, keep your shoulders straight and open, tuck your chin slightly.

You may use a zafu on its side for support or a specially constructed seiza bench.

I find sitting this way is an excellent tool in assisting me to get in deep touch with the feminine within. It is difficult to feel aggressive feelings in this pose. Much like gassho assists us in opening ourselves to compassion and releases anger, seiza opens us to receptivity and relaxes defenses.

As always, when you sit, sit with dignity.

25

Ten Ox-Herding Pictures

Stage Seven

Sunday, January 15, 2006

Introduction

In the dharma there is no duality; the Ox is the foundation.
It may be compared to the rabbit and the snare;
it is expressed in the difference between fish and weir.
Like gold coming from ore,
like the moon emerging from behind the clouds.
The Single Way of cold light has been shining
ever since the time of Ion beyond the kalpas.

Verse

You have mounted the ox
and already reached your home in the mountains.
The ox is gone and the person has nothing more to do.
Though the morning sun has already risen three bamboo lengths,
he dreams on.
The whip and the halter, no longer of use, are hung up in the stall.

So Daiho:

Opening my eyes this morning, I thought of you. My dogs, Tripper and Pepper waited patiently, the coffee was made, bows made, the incense was lit. Nothing here is apart from one another. You, I, dogs, coffee, incense, and all of the actions are the same without any distinction. Distinction is an illusion of mind.

These things were always there and will always be here. And more, there really is no here or there, then and now. We call this our original nature. Our original nature is our continuous nature, our perpetual nature. Once understood, once attained, we realize it's true nature.

So, then, of what use language? So, then, what use zafus, robes, dog leashes, coffee?

May All Beings Be Free From Suffering

26

Practice - poem

Sunday, January 15, 2006

If I am originally water and I gradually become wave, what do I do?
If I am then sky and I suddenly become bird, how do I see sky?

27

Ten Ox-Herding Pictures

Stage Eight

Monday, January 16, 2006

Introduction

Ordinary feelings have fallen away, thoughts of holiness are all empty.

We should not linger where there is Buddha;

we should pass quickly by where there is no Buddha.

If we do not stick to either,

It will be difficult for a thousand eyes to perceive us.

For myriad birds to carry flowers is a shame all around.

Verse

Whip, tether, person and ox - all are empty.

The blue sky spreads out far and wide, it cannot be communicated.

On a red-hot oven, how can there be any place for snow?

Having come this far, you understand the intention of the patriarchs.

So Daiho:

We chant the Wisdom Heart Sutra, all bowing with the sound of the bell. We adjust the flowing robes and sit facing the wall. We rise and walk, feeling each footfall, each stiff muscle relax. We sit again. We sip our tea so graciously served. We listen to the Dharma, incomparably profound and minutely subtle. When we do this awake, there is no room for even a single thought, not a single feeling. The oven is, indeed, hot.

Practicing like this there is no practice and no practitioner. There is simple awareness in motion. The tools are just tools and are no longer necessary. But because we are buddhas we continue: through time and space there we are; one, all, none.

Just so, we get up in the morning and greet the day. We say hello to the kitty, the dogs, the coffee pot. We sit zazen, we wash our faces, clean our teeth. We go to work, driving, walking, running, sitting, eating, talking. Done fully and completely, there is no room for wobbles.

28

Ten Ox-Herding Pictures

Stage Nine

Tuesday, January 17, 2006

Introduction

It is originally pure and clean without a speck of dust clinging.
He observes the flourishing and dying of form
while remaining in the silence of no-action.
This is not the same as illusion; what need is there for striving or
planning?
The water is blue and the mountains green;
he sits and watches phenomena take form and decay.

Verse

Having come back to the origin and returned to the source,
you see that you have expended efforts in vain.
What could be superior to becoming blind and deaf
in this very moment?
Inside the hermitage,
you do not see what is in front of the hermitage.

The water flows of itself and the flowers are naturally red.

So Daiho:

The bodhisattvas whisper in our ear. We see poverty. We see war. We see cruelty and illness, sickness and death. We see our neighbors stealing, lying, cheating, and swindling. We see the world manipulating as if it is OK because we are, after all, just putting a positive "spin" on things. We see this all as one side of the human coin. And the bodhisattvas whisper.

We are here to attain a clear mind then step out into the universe to assist all beings. We are here to help. To save. To nurture. To witness. To do what is there to be done.

There should be no distinctions here: just wash the dishes, write to your congressman, talk to your neighbor. No better or worse, higher or lower, just the simple and clear expression of buddha in action. Saving a fly from death is the same as saving a man from execution. It is our true nature to witness.

So here it is: our practice is to destroy the stored assumptions we carry around on our backs, these multiply colored filters through which we distort our perception and thus, skew our thoughts, feelings and behavior. Our practice is to develop a clear mind. To perceive without history and distinction, without distorted thought and feeling, then to seamlessly behave according to what is there to do.

Our time on the cushion is time with the ultimate therapist who cures us and sends us on our way.

As the present moment yields all causes and conditions before, lizards now speak and slime walks. The combustion of creation is settled in form. And in process. And in form. And in process.

In this place, beginning and end have no meaning.

29

The Other Side of One

Tuesday, January 17, 2006

This morning I awake to see I killed an old man last night. Strapped his ass down and filled him full of poison. I also stood outside the death chamber as a silent witness. And slept in my bed, comfortable and thoughtless as to what I was doing.

When we say we are one, what do we mean? When we say we are all buddha-nature waiting to crack out of that vast emptiness we could call a cosmic egg, what does this mean?

If we are all one, then we are all killing, all witnessing, all crying, all starving, all sleeping, all fucking, shitting, eating, and whatever else we human beings, mice, worms, cats and dogs do. So, then, what is our responsibility?

When you get up this morning, that question is your practice.

30

Ten Ox-Herding Pictures

Stage Ten

Wednesday, January 18, 2006

Introduction

> He closes the thatched gate to his hermitage
> so that even the thousand sages do not know of him.
> He buries the light of his own knowing
> and goes against the tracks left by former sages.
> Carrying a gourd, he enters the marketplace;
> holding his staff, he returns home,
> Bestowing Buddhahood on barkeeps and fishmongers.

Verse

> Shoeless and bare-chested he enters the marketplace;
> He is daubed with earth and ashes, and a smile fills his face.
> Making no use of the secrets of gods and wizards,
> He causes withered trees to bloom.

So Daiho:

When we are buddhas there is no need for the signs and symbols, the shoes and the robes, of the Buddha. There is no need for sticks and whisks, special words, or bells and incense. Transformative process is like this.

Our presence is enough. The way we open a door. The way we smile. The way we invite. The way we say no. Each speaks as silence is to thunder.

When we are buddhas there is no Zen apart from us. Our way is Zen, regardless of how Zen came and went in the past. So we set out on our own way, free of the trappings of our Teacher, free of the trappings of the Buddha himself.

In so doing, what was once a stiff, old teaching or a varicose-veined Temple, is now living and vibrant. This is dialectic. This is life.

We still wear our robes. We still shave our heads. We still light our incense and make bows. There is a deep and profound difference between habits and manifestations. Just as there is a difference between a candle without a flame and a candle burning bright.

In this so-called "Stage" we are understood as beings in full expression of Buddha-nature. Our each action is a seamless expression of Buddha-dharma. Our bodies are the body of the Buddha. The notion of these stages happening as sequential events is very misleading. While it is true, in my opinion, that in order for seeds to sprout, the ground of our being must first be tilled by both life and death and a true practice, there is no moment within which the Buddha is not present within each of us. So in each moment an eye may open and light shine forth. Our continuous practice is to assist us, so to speak, in keeping our eye open regardless of the time of day.

31

Awake?

Thursday, January 19, 2006

When we open our eyes in the morning and get out of bed, we are not necessarily awake. We might be thinking of what we have to get done this morning or what we must do this afternoon or this evening. We might be feeling a bit tired or grumpy or our muscles might need a stretch. We might smell the coffee in the air or the car exhaust as we leave our homes to go to work. We might see a flower and say to ourselves, that's an awfully pretty flower!

But this is only awake to our thoughts, feelings, and sensations. It is not being awake.

Being awake is being before the thoughts, the feelings, the sensations. Being awake is seeing directly with a clear mind reflecting only what is there, and in so doing becomes us. Thought is just thought. Feeling is just feeling. Smell is just smell. Flower is just flower.

If we open our eyes like this, our Buddha-nature opens with them. Our Buddha-nature and the thought is one. Our Buddha-nature and our feeling is one. Our Buddha-nature and the flower are one.

Does it matter?

Second guessing, concern, worry...all take us away from being fully present. When we are not fully present, we are living in something that has no foundation, no reality. Thoughts, feelings, and sensations have no reality of their own. How can we be present with the flower or our wife, husband, child, co-worker, client, work, when we are only with their idea?

So, this is our practice: be with what is there without regard for what we "think" of it, "feel" about it, or "sense" about it, and more, without regard for the next moment.

32

Moving Practice

Friday, January 20, 2006

There is Zen of Stillness and there is Zen of Movement. In the Zendo we practice both: zazen and kinhin. There is a reason for this. We talk so much about the ideas of Zen. We talk about the paramitas, the precepts, sitting zazen, etc. In spite of all the words, Zen is not about them. The talk is about walking the walk. In this case, the walk is literal.

Today is the last day of my modified training schedule which includes a longish run/walk. Also today I will work my legs with weights. Beginning Monday morning my workouts will change, upping the volume to several sets of heavy weight Monday through Friday each day targeting a major muscle group: chest/back, arms/shoulders, legs, chest/back, arms/shoulders. I will do a short treadmill run following each of those workouts and on Tuesdays and Thursdays go outside for a longer run. Saturday will be rest and Sunday will be my Long Slow Distance run day.

Daily hard and vigorous exercise is a good Zen practice. We enter this practice with an open mind, accepting of our body and its limitations, as well as its need to be stressed. We were built to move. Our muscles and cardiovascular system demands it; our digestive system works better with it; and our central nervous system has an opportunity to integrate with our total body.

It is challenging for us to begin and stay with this practice. We find all sorts of reasons not to do it: time, pain, lack of inclination, ideology, fear. The same reasons we use not to sit zazen. Or do other practices which will nurture both our bodies and the planet.

Let me encourage each of you to begin a moving practice today. Walk, bike, lift, play: it really doesn't matter. Just do this practice with right concentration and right effort. Being mindful in each movement we increase our awareness of, and integration with, our mind and body. As we progress we will feel stronger, healthier, and more confident.

33

The Flavor of Kindness

Tuesday, January 24, 2006

Each of you brings energy into the world. Some bring angry energy, some happy energy, some sad energy, and each of these energies are expressed through our affect and behavior. It is reflected in the choices we make. People see us and see reflected in us the energy we are communicating. In this way, the energy travels.

It is important for us to understand that which energy is being expressed is a result of the thoughts we have and that these thoughts are based on perception, though in most cases a perception distorted by our memory. Our memory forms a virtual encyclopedia of senses, experiences, concepts; it is our universe and is kept active by a little monkey that seems to delight in stirring the cauldron.

The thing is, we have the ability to see directly without the cauldron of history. In so doing, we see without distortion. We see without our history. In such cases we see exactly and precisely what is there with nothing added; no discrimination, no like, no dislike, no name. When we see this way only Buddha-nature is communicated in our affect and our behavior.

I often rant about the fall of civilization, both western and eastern. I rant about materialism and hedonism. I rant about Wal-Mart and McDonalds, about obesity and (to borrow from another religious tradition) the other deadly sins. These rants contain an expression of affect and are a behavior. They betray, to a certain extent, a standard and a judgment regarding a deviation from that standard.

Where does this standard come from? Is a moment of the cushion or on a walk or in an activity which reveals a clear perception of the buddha within that standard? And if so, what do we do with it?

As we allow this buddha to arise and manifest itself in us, we are manifesting the excellences of our Original Nature. We are the paramitas: generosity, patience, precepts, vigor, meditation, and wisdom. We know that on the one hand, all things are the dharma and are expressions of the universe in process. We know on the other hand that some of these expressions are conducive to the discovery of harmony and compassion, whereas others are distractions, poisons, if you will, that take us away from a compassionate heart.

It comes to intent. Intent is key to the production of karma. If our rant is for the sake of bringing beings closer to the attainment of perfection, then it is one thing, a noble purpose. If on the other hand the rant is for our personal gratification, to simply "vent" or to prove another is wrong, corrupt, a failure, whatever, then this is a sin, a misstep along our path.

All of our affect, all of our behavior should thus be evaluated by us as we get up from bed and go through our day. Our practice is to bring our buddha-nature into the world through our compassionate action. To do this we need to recognize our intent and act for the correct purposes. To do this, we need to develop a strong zazen practice. Time with ourselves on the cushion in quiet stillness and serene reflection is a direct path to clarity.

34

Perfection

Sunday, January 29, 2006

At the conclusion of the Wisdom Heart Sutra we chant "Gate, gate, gate, paragate, parasamgate, Bodhi Svaha!" Or, Gone, gone, gone to the other shore, attained the other shore having never left, Awaken. Hooray!" Gate, pronounced gah-tay, is the sino-japanaese word for paramita. We translate paramita as "perfection" or "excellence." It is understood to be a reference to attainment. So, this dharani, (short mantra) is saying that attainment is something we already possess, even though we strive to attain it. The "other shore," attainment, enlightenment, is with us right now, right here. It is us. It is the universe.

The combining of qualities and notions such as "shore," "perfection," "excellence," "crossing," never leaving, attaining, etc. is a linguistic way of picking up a hammer and cracking ourselves over the head. All one, yet different. This shore, this moment, this understanding is the same as that moment, that shore, that understanding. And there is no real movement from one to the other because they exist in the same time and in the same space simultaneously.

Our effort to be good people, to sit strong Zen, is nothing more than the sweat equity involved in growing a tree knowing that the fruit, the branches, the roots, and shade of that tree already exist in the seed, in the ground, in the air, and in the water. We still make the effort. We still till the soil, plant the seed and nurse the plant. Yet when we do so with open eyes, effort is bliss.

35

Why?

Monday, January 30, 2006

To sit each morning and each evening is an excellent way to begin and close your day. Stillness allows us to gather ourselves, calm our minds and bodies, and form the necessary mind to enter the world and leave the world as buddhas. The act of lighting a candle, lighting incense, bowing, then sitting down on the cushion is a profound act of discipline and dedication. In this small theater for no one to see, there is just you. Placing attention on our breath, allowing what is present to be present, and accepting the gifts of that moment regardless of their qualities, is of enormous benefit. But even if it wasn't of any benefit at all, we should still sit in stillness.

Why?

36

Zen Tango

Tuesday, January 31, 2006

This morning I wrote a short note in my Yahoo 360 blog:

We are at the end of the first month of the new year. Most of us have, by now gotten used to the 06, then again, there is me. I am slow to notice the outward manifestation of change. I think that is because I am change itself, mostly dwelling in the moment, not looking at the horizon so much to see where I am. On the other hand, maybe 05 and 06 do not really exist. Maybe it is only this key pressing to making contact that exists, but only for a moment. It is an odd sort of dance this absolute and relative tango.

In Uji, one of Master Dogen's Shobogenzo essays, he uses a boat slipping along against the shore as a way of teaching the interrelation of Time and Being. And there is an old koan that addresses a similar issue: two monks pointing to a flagpole arguing (always two monks arguing). Which is moving, the flag or the wind?

We have talked about the two truths of Buddhism, the absolute and the relative. These truths are not independent. Buddha taught that all things are interdependent, this includes time, being, and space. Our "moment" consciousness interacts with our "ever" consciousness. When the interaction is choppy and stilted, we have a dance that is in dukkha. When we have an interaction that is easy and flowing, seamless, then we have a gracious waltz, no suffering. We do a sort of tango with these dances. Sometimes easy, sometimes difficult.

It is important to recognize they are both dances: dukkha and the absence of dukkha, samsara and nirvana, relative and absolute, time and being. Both exist, both do not exist. Only together is the universe made. Only together is it understood. Only together is it attained.

So, what does this mean in terms of Zen Living? Do not let your mind be an obstacle.

37

Love

Tuesday, February 7, 2006

It is dark outside. And cold. The desert does not hold the heat of the sun. I am sitting by my bedroom window thinking about the next few days. Visiting our daughter will be a delight. Her dissertation defense will be stressful. They always are. My hope is that we will get through it, enjoy the process as best we can, then celebrate and come home.

Moments are what they are. Sometimes good, sometimes not so good, sometimes a real pain in the ass. Still, being present is all that we have really. Yesterday and tomorrow do not exist. It is pointless to fret over what was or over what might be. So, in this very moment what I experience is love.

My breath enters my body and my breath leaves my body. I am still. My heart is warm. I love.

When we have love in every present moment what else is there?

No room for hate. No room for fear. No room for worry. Just a deep and abiding love.

I have faith in this universe and its processes. It is way larger than me. And yet there I am in it. Part of it, all of it, none of it.

There are those who would look around and see all the death and destruction, the hate and fear, and say, "what an awful, terrible world." There are others who look at the same things and see the human heart beating, overcoming great odds, and still loving. The will to life and love are powerful. They are the currents of the universe. And while we clash, we also embrace. While we kill, we also save. My sense is that the balances are always tipped in favor of life and love.

Spread the love, one being at a time.

38

Political Zen

Sunday, February 12, 2006

Lately I have posted a number of political messages. Some may argue these are "off topic." I wonder. It seems to me that Zen Living is political living. The question we each face as we rise every morning is how are we to steer ourselves in the world. Zen informs us of that steerage. Zen is the compass we use, a tool, if you will, of discovery. We investigate ourselves through Zazen and through this practice realize ourselves, so to speak, in the universe. Zen in this sense is not an individual activity, but a dynamic interaction with everything in all places. It is in this sense that Zen becomes political. Politics, according to Webster, is the art or science of government or governing. Law and policy are nothing more than a group's precepts stated as rules and guidelines. Precepts then become political statements.

When I take refuge in the Buddha, the Dharma, and the Sangha, what does this mean? When I vow not to kill, steal, poison my mind, what do these mean? They are not precepts for only us as individuals, they are precepts for us as members of a group. They are our policy, our governance. And, in this case, I argue, our group is the family of man.

When we engage the precepts we are engaged in a process of living. How are we to effect the precepts in the world? This process is a political one. When we see killing we must stand opposed to it. When we see a violation of human rights, we must stand opposed to it. When we see a corporation poisoning the air or the water, we must stand opposed to it. As a Sangha, this becomes a political activity.

If we approach Zen only as a means of self-improvement or of enlightenment for ourselves alone, we are taking a wrong approach. Such a practice will only end in disaster and frustration. Zen is about neither.

39

Witness and Participant

Monday, February 13, 2006

Each day we are both witnesses and participants in our universe. As interactive players we both learn and teach simultaneously. So each day we should look to ourselves and ask, what do we want to teach? What do we wish to learn?

The most simple and routine tasks are often the best examples and offer the greatest teachings. Feeding the baby, feeding the dog, taking a bath, brushing our teeth, saying hello to our neighbor, driving our car, doing our work, preparing our food, eating, using the bathroom, making love, sitting zazen: teachers all. In each of these, it seems to me the most valuable teaching and learning is presence.

Can we be present when feeding the dog? Do we really see our neighbor? Do we feel the food as we prepare it, recall the various hands and lives it is? As we join our partner, can we allow ourselves to drop away and be union itself?

These take practice. These take deliberate effort. A seeming contradiction: practice-effort and simultaneous witness-participation. But is only seeming. When we first learn anything, we are painfully and acutely aware to our "learning" state. As we accomplish and integrate the teaching, we become the teaching and become less aware of "learning" or "doing." The flow from subject to object, relative to absolute, and back again, becomes increasingly seamless. Soon we notice there is no flow at all.

I invite you to be a witness and a participant in our universe today.

40

A Valentine

Tuesday, February 14, 2006

May each of your hearts be warm and open.

In a world where the news is as an acid to our connections with one another, I ask that we hold hands in prayer. Love is the antidote to hatred. There is no more powerful antidote to its corrosive effects. Yet, to love requires courage and faith. Courage to love those that hate us; faith that in the process of loving, life will continue to blossom. If we are worried that our individual flame will be snuffed out, we are lost.

We must look deeply at this hate, see its fundamental cause as fear, and assuage that fear. In its place, we offer peace and compassionate regard. We offer support and nurturance. We do not feed the delusion of separation; we feed the truth of oneness and interdependence. Who here is a separate, fully self-sustaining individual who has "made it" with no help or support or teaching or encouragement or nurturance from others?

It is so easy to talk this talk. My challenge is for each of us to walk it.

Another form of kinhin.

41

So, you want to learn Zen!

Monday, February 20, 2006

When we first consider Zen, what are we considering? What do we see in this Zen? Why are we looking in the first place? What does it all mean?

Typically, westerners are curious. Maybe they heard meditation is good for them. Maybe they want to become better people. Maybe they feel stressed and have been told meditation is a stress management tool. Perhaps they have not had so good experiences in their Church or Synagogue. Maybe they read a book or two, possibly by Alan Watts, D. T. Suzuki, Phillip Kapleau-roshi or Shunryu Suzuki-roshi. Whatever. They come to Zen to meet a need.

Then they find themselves in a Zen Center. In the Center they are greeted by bald headed guys in black robes wearing brown or black bibs. What's up with that? They are asked not to talk much. Not to read much. Not to do anything loud. Then they are asked to stand, bow, put their hands together as if they were praying. There are statues, incense, bells. They are asked to chant in a foreign language. They are asked to sit on a cushion facing a wall for an awfully long time, stand and walk in an odd sort of way, in a circle, going nowhere, just to get back to their cushion and sit down with pained knees facing the wall again. Moving is frowned upon. they are asked not to scratch themselves unless necessary. Oh yeah, this is the path to stress reduction.

Zen is all and none of the above.

Zen is about discipline. It is about self-discovery. It is about moral behavior. It is about developing the ability and willingness to be compassionate, kind, forgiving, inclusive, non-judgmental. And somewhere in that mix, Zen is boring.

We sit with our legs folded facing a wall doing nothing. We are asked to place our attention on our breath, or our "hara," or nowhere at all. So, we just sit there. We want to move. We want someone to teach us something and by this, I mean, tell us something, you know, TALK to us! Mention a book, an idea, something! But instead, we just sit there. We think. We feel. We wonder just what in the hell ever got into us.

Sometime or other a bell is "invited" to ring, and we are finally allowed to get up. Only to sit down again and listen to some "Teacher" as he or she talks to us. Now this is more like it! Language, words, ideas! Great! Then he says, forget everything I have said. Say what?

Of course, none of this makes any sense.

It doesn't. It isn't supposed to. The whole affair is intended to get you out of your mind. Zen is about experience, not thought. We often confuse the two. As if thinking about riding a bike is the same as actually riding the bike. There is no substitute for the sheer act of sitting down and quietly doing nothing. This doing nothing is, it turns out, quite a dynamic process. It involves our bodies, minds, and feelings. It involves history. It involves our desires, our intentions, our worst fears. And there is nowhere to go to get away from any of them. Nowhere.

42

Emptiness

Tuesday, February 21, 2006

This morning, I would like to talk about emptiness. It seems we are often confused by this term. Shunyata simply means empty of something. It does not mean non-existence. So, when we see ourselves as "empty," we see we are without a fixed self, a self that does not change. Shunyata points to our interdependence for existence in both time and space. We are, in fact, a matrix that is infinite. It is just a matter of perspective that allows us to "see" a collection of molecules we call a "body" and a great interlocking chain of events (or causes) that allow us to become conscious of a "self."

So, when we pinch ourselves, we hurt, yet we "know" this pain is "empty" of an independent and permanent existence, just as are our bodies, minds, and feelings. We still feel pain. We still exist in the world and are responsible for our actions and the actions of others.

We cannot use "emptiness" and "no-self" as a quiet excuse to do nothing.

43

Crime

Tuesday, February 21, 2006

For those of you who are thinking about committing a crime tonight, please re-consider. Violence against people and property is never a good idea. Health and well-being are precious and cannot be replaced. Property comes and goes and never brings us the satisfaction we imagine it will. For those of you who will be victims of crime tonight, before you seek an eye for an eye, ask yourself if you want the world to be blind.

I have both committed crime and been a victim of crime. In my life I have stolen, lied, cheated and killed. I have also been robbed and assaulted. I have been shot. I have been molested. Being on both sides of the highway is a challenge sometimes, but it certainly gives one some perspective on behavior. I know when I was a kid and stole from stores, it felt good and I was able to get candy, chips, sodas and cigarettes. I wish I had never stolen, especially the cigarettes. I have lied. I have told people things that were not true in order (I think) to protect myself from loss or disapproval or some other imagined thing. I have cheated, inflated my income or deflated my income depending on the paperwork. I have killed people in combat, one was a friend who got in the line of fire. An awful tragedy which tore my heart in half and caused me to lose faith in myself. As a victim, I've been robbed several times; house broken into, things taken. I was assaulted by a friend, held at knifepoint, and another time punched. When I was younger, as a child skipping school, I was sexually propositioned by a man in a public restroom. As a young adult, I was sexually assaulted by a man. Oh my, the list is long.

Today I see that these things, awful as they might be, are no longer real. They exist only in my memory; a memory now being assaulted by a disease related to my combat experience. I am comfortable with this. I have seen clearly the nature of the universe. All things come and go. What is important is the process.

A priest now, I have taken solemn vows to be with all beings in their suffering as long as it takes to bring all beings out of suffering. An infinite task and one not to be taken lightly. Tonight, there are people in harm's way, soldiers, poor people, starving people, people deathly ill. Tonight, there are people who are going to die and there are people who are going to be born. It is our work to make this planet both a safer place and a better place for people to live. There is enough suffering, we need not add to it with our selfishness and our self-centered needs.

When we take up the practice of Zen we enter into this vast stream, this eternal process of life and as we enter we open our eyes. It takes great courage to do this and to also stay in the stream.

What will you do tomorrow?

44

The Challenge of Zazen

Thursday, February 23, 2006

This morning, I lit sticks of incense and said a prayer for all of those in the world who were suffering. It seems from the morning's news, there's a lot of that going around. Mudslides, wars, violence against individuals, communities, and religious buildings. I take a breath and sit down on my cushion, turn and face the wall. My hands rest gently in the cosmic mudra, left hand cradled in the right, thumbs lightly touching. I feel the presence of the universe wrap me like a blanket, creating a nest of safety and security. This, however, is not Zazen. It is just a good feeling.

It takes work to move against this, to press out the warmth, to lift off the blanket and open myself to the larger processes of life and death. To be one with the universe means some very challenging things. It means we do not hide from the suffering of others. It means we do not have the luxury of being overwhelmed by the global nature of the task or its seeming futility. It means we have an obligation to behave just now, right here, in this moment and perhaps exceeding our capacity. It means we must open our eyes and experience the universe as it is, rather than as some sugar-coated pill we would like it to be. I have heard it said that science discovers and describes what is, and religion discovers and describes what ought to be. Where is the bridge?

Look in the mirror.

45

Darwin

Friday, February 24, 2006

The trouble with violence is that it is too often used instead of compassion, understanding, and a willingness to work out a solution to a problem. It becomes easy. It becomes an habit. It becomes automatic. When this happens, and we develop a rationale that enables the habit, then we lose civilization. We become addicts who can't stand to hear the word, "no."

Violence disallows a long view, it demands a short view. Violence does not consider others, it only considers ourselves. Violence is me first, you last. Violence is a statement of egoistic priority.

Non-violence demands a long view, it requires patience, a willingness to accept difference, and a willingness to think. Non-violence puts others first and ourselves last. Non-violence is a statement of mutual aid as priority. Non-violence is civilization.

For decades the social Darwinists have suggested dominance through violence, fierce competition, and placing winning between the eyes, is a natural condition. Yet these social scientists often fail to see the most basic elements of survival.

The fittest survives. The question is, what determines "fitness"? Is it strength? Is it the willingness to use force? I doubt it. These are short-term and short-sighted quick fixes to meet our impatient needs. I suggest fitness is manifest in compassion. In our willingness to understand others. And in our willingness to provide mutual aid. In this sense, the fittest are those who are the most caring and compassionate among us. The fittest are those willing to set aside their own needs for the sake and well-being of all.

We survive because we care for each other. We survive because we are interconnected with each other. We thrive when we celebrate that care and that interconnection.

Let each one of us find a way today to be of benefit to others.

46

Change

Saturday, February 25, 2006

If you are at work reading this, or at school, please consider that this moment is not a dress rehearsal for some future moment of life. This is your life. If there is something you do not like about this moment, as Thoreau once said, change it.

If our immediate thought is, "I can't", then you can't. You, yourself, are a hindrance to your change. If you say, "OK, tomorrow, I will begin." Then you are living in a delusion. This moment is it. Only this moment.

Now is the time. Now.

47

One

Monday, February 27, 2006

My wife just asked me what I was doing. My head was bowed as was gently stroking my less than functional left elbow sitting at the computer. Nothing but the soft whirring of the motor cooling the machine and the bright light of the morning sun. I said I was preparing to type my morning message. She asked, "Oh, you don't have a book of them?"

In truth, I do not. I try to settle myself a little, visit that interior world with the morning light at my window, and wait. When interior and exterior come together, I begin to type and the message takes shape, form, if you will, and there it is. It is a process I have trusted for several decades now.

Spirituality, though the term is often confusing and confused, is like that. Interior meets exterior, exterior meets interior, through the breath. At some point, the two are seen for what they truly are: expressions of the oneness of process. The stages are artificial, imposed by Small Mind as it attempts to discriminate in order to understand. In this process, Big Mind is not seen, just as we sometimes cannot see the forest for the trees. Spiritual practice uses the breath to bring these two Minds together, or rather, enable us to see them as they actually are.

Breathe easy, allow the Universe and You to resolve your true nature. We are One.

48

Being Peace

Tuesday, February 28, 2006

This past Sunday I talked about the Four Noble Truths during my Dharma Talk at the Zen Center. Every once in a while, I think it is good to be reminded of these truths, especially the Fourth Truth, that of the Eightfold Noble Path.

The thing is, these truths speak to us about the virtue of moderation. The truth is rarely, if ever, in extremes, suggesting that there is great truth in the maxim, "too much of a good thing is a bad thing."

When we talk about "right" in the Eightfold Noble Path, we are actually talking about "correct." In this case, correct means balanced, moderate, middle: leaning to neither extreme. So, "Right Speech": is speech that is moderate, not extreme, not inflammatory. Also, it would be speech that is intended to heal people, to nurture them, rather than assault them or diminish them.

Moderation and balance are often difficult to attain and maintain. We live in a world with extremes challenging us on a daily, often moment-to-moment basis. Our practice is to establish and maintain a certain balance in the midst of it. Difficult indeed.

Yet, when the storm comes (and we know that it will) where is our heart/mind? It should be in calm abiding. When the storm comes, practice. Place your attention on the thing, take it in, let it be. It will resolve of its own accord. This is our faith. Feelings and thoughts and behaviors are all temporary. Everything comes and goes. Even the worst of things. However, if we maintain our Middle Way in the midst of it all, we can be a model of peace and compassion to those being tossed about in the process.

Being a model in this sense is offering hope to others. Not bad for an ordinary person.

49

Extremes?

Wednesday, March 1, 2006

Someone suggested I might be considered an "extremist." I smiled deeply as I read it. I wonder. Perhaps. I don't consider myself an extremist. I see myself as an able mediator, a negotiator who seeks balance and something for everyone. My views are informed by both my experience and my values, intertwined as they always are through time and process.

My views on violence are informed by witnessing violence against my mother, brother, and myself by my father. They are informed by my experience as a combat infantryman in Vietnam who hunted human beings for a living and was wounded in the process. They are informed by thirty years of clinical work with trauma survivors in mental hospitals and outpatient clinics. I see no value in violence. None.

However, I am also informed by the fact that there are violent people in the world who would do harm to me and my family, my community, my nation, my world. This is a fact of life. And so, we are left with a question. How do we protect ourselves from those who would cause us harm without ourselves causing harm?

It is at this juncture that we need to take a breath. Because we are so bombarded with images of violence, the news casts threats of violence with such a wide net, that we seem to think we are each in imminent danger and should act as if the world were a hostile and violent place. This is simply not true. Yes, there is violence in the world. No, not every person poses a threat of harm. Not every stranger is an enemy lurking in wait to attack us. For every act of violence, even in the Middle East, there are countless acts of selfless heroism, attempts to help and care and nurture those in harm's way. We see the bomb's damage but fail to see the hundreds of people picking up the pieces and loving those who are injured.

You see, as I see it, most commentators only go so far as to justify violence with the fact that violence exists. But if we are value driven, and our value is sanctifying of life, and the nurturance and protection of life, then (it seems to me) we must go farther. It is in this "going father" that most of us get hopelessly lost or confused. We seem unwilling to step outside the cultural, conventional wisdom box and see with unfettered eyes.

So, how do we protect ourselves without causing harm?

An extreme position would be to run away. Flee the situation. A less extreme position would be to offer assistance to those wishing to cause harm. We might consider listening to them, deeply listening. Most anger is caused by perceived injury or threat. What is the injury? What is the threat? Is there something we can do to help? Is the anger caused by an unbalanced mind? Are there therapies or medications that can help? Do people have enough food? Care? Housing? Do they have hope? Are they being treated fairly?

We take Four Great Vows daily: However innumerable all beings are, I vow to save them all; however inexhaustible my delusions are, I vow to extinguish them all; however immeasurable the Dharma teachings are, I vow to master them all; and however endless the Buddha's Way is, I vow to follow it completely.

These vows do not exclude a single being, not one from here to eternity. It does not matter whether they are ugly, fat, skinny, kind, or killers. These vows do not exclude delusions that keep us smug and healthy, they include all delusions including ones that suggest some people are just plain, not like us and therefore unworthy of our care and love. These vows do not exclude Dharma teachings that are impractical or uncomfortable or opposed to conventional wisdom. Lastly, these vows are not for just this moment, they are for all moments in every context and in every location.

Extreme? Perhaps. Our vows ask us to follow a middle path through the maze life presents us, leaning not too far this way or that. Still, values must drive our choices, rather than what we knee jerk think should be done. We must use our intelligence, our compassion, our resources, and our wisdom to make a better world. It is our work. It's what we do as human beings.

50

Who Am I?

Thursday, March 2, 2006

What is the "higher" truth? Does God exist? Is there a Heaven? A Hell? Where do we fit in along the way? Was there a beginning? Will there be an end? Who am I? What am I? How should I live my life? How should I treat my friends, my family, strangers? Where do we go to get the answers to these questions?

Some would say we should go to Church or Synagogue or Mosque or Temple. I would agree. A good religious center would then take us and sit us down and ask us to take a backward step. A good religious center would not give us answers to these questions, instead they would invite us to examine ourselves, deeply examine ourselves. Of course, in the process of this examination they would offer us tools.

Liturgy is such a tool. Means of practice, such as daily rituals, meditation, chanting, are such tools. Prayer in its many colored and textured varieties are such tools. But these are not the answers themselves. It is a mistake to think that because you bow and light incense you are connecting to anything. It is a mistake to think that because you put on a prayer shawl or a robe that you are getting closer to God, being like Jesus, or becoming a Buddha. These are important practices and they will orient you, but they are not the thing itself.

The thing itself comes from inside out. It is in your heart/mind.

The backward step is, of course, a step into stillness. A step into your "still small voice." Not just listening to that voice but enjoying that voice. You and that voice are one, just as you and your God are one, just as you and Jesus are one or you and Buddha are one. This One, regardless of name, is there whether we feel it or not, see it or not, experience it or not. The questions I asked at the beginning are our invitations to discover this One.

It is now your turn to take this backward step. Be still.

51

On Being Soft

Friday, March 3, 2006

Maintaining a sense of interest in the well-being of your partner may be in your own best interest in the long run. When we speak and (otherwise) behave with our partner with loving kindness, we soften ourselves and our partners, making our union a more joyous and comfortable one. On the other hand, when we speak to our partners with anger and behave in a hostile, controlling manner, we harden ourselves and our partners, making our relationship brittle.

It seems that these truths may be deeper and more concrete than we might expect. Researchers suggest that anger and hostile interactions with our partners contributes to coronary atherosclerosis, hardening of the arteries.

"In a study of 150 couples, mostly in their 60s, researchers found that women who behaved in a hostile manner during marital disputes were more likely to have atherosclerosis, especially if their husbands were also hostile."

"In men, hostility -- their own or their wives -- was not related to atherosclerosis. However, men who behaved in a dominating or controlling manner -- or whose wives behaved in that way -- were more likely to have clogged coronary arteries." says a study from the University of Utah as reported by Reuters Health News.

A gentle way is a healthy way, it would seem.

"The only group of men that had very little atherosclerosis were those where both they and their wives were able to talk about a disagreement without being controlling at all," (Dr. Timothy) Smith said. "So the absence of a power play in the conversation seemed to be heart protective for men," he concluded.

My sense here is that perception plays a major role in this. How we perceive, leads to how we think, feel, and respond behaviorally. Even if there is no outward behavioral response, perceiving oneself as being in the presence of a hostile and controlling person may increase our risk. Interesting. So, what are we to do?

My practice tells me that understanding process without becoming caught in process is a key to dealing with this. If we were to clearly see ourselves as simply being there, with no investment one way or the other as to outcome, taking a long view, a hopeful view, of the interaction, we would be much better off. Too often we are caught in the minute points of an argument. Who said what with what sort of tone, intending what to whom. Or some equal variant on this theme. We wish to be understood; we wish to be accepted. We wish to be agreed with, heard, validated, something. Yet, our partner keeps hammering away.

Our goal should be to be present in these arguments without ratcheting them up. The best way to do this, I think, is to make yourself available in that moment to listen deeply to your partner. Love her/him in their pain or their confusion or their anger. This requires us to be willing to set aside our own agenda and needs.

To do this we must possess and maintain a faith that our needs will eventually be addressed. My experience is that these "needs" are almost always immediate and responsive to our partner's request to have their needs met. In other words, our "needs" are really more about our unwillingness to give up ourselves to our partners than an actual need itself.

Here's the thing: needs come and go. Why be bothered by the tit-for-tat of power and control? Especially now that we have some evidence that it is hazardous to our health.

52

Mindful Silence

Saturday, March 4, 2006

My suggestion for today is to spend the day in mindful silence. It is a good practice.

Speak only when spoken to in as limited and gentle way as possible. When we do this, we are placing ourselves in the position of being open to our lives in a way that doesn't happen when we are busy with our minds and mouths.

Knowing that we are not speaking, we can listen more closely. Listening more closely enables a more intimate connection to be made to our world. It is in this intimacy that profound change occurs.

53

50's

Sunday, March 5, 2006

This evening, I was thinking about what I could possibly write about. I thought about this:

50 Simple things to do:

Turn off lights when you are not using them.
Use energy saving bulbs.
Cook as little as possible, use cold foods in the summer.
Buy in quantities, then parcel into smaller portions for storage and later use.
Use a half-shot glass of bleach in a spray water bottle instead of a cleanser to disinfect counter surfaces.
Flush the toilet less times per day.
Turn off the tap when not actually using the water.
Set your water heater on medium rather than high.
Bike rather than drive.
Walk rather than bike.
Park as far away from the entrance of a store as you possibly can then walk.
Eat six times a day, but smaller amounts.
Eat fruit.
Eat veggies.
Drink juice.

Drink lots of water.

Make as much from scratch as you can.

Enjoy yourself.

Each day for a week eat something you've not tried before.

Eat more nuts.

Smile as often as possible, especially when you don't feel like it.

Tell your partner you love them.

Show your partner your love in non-verbal ways.

Volunteer.

Work less than you think you should.

Turn off your cell phone for a day.

Begin a diary.

Stop writing in your diary.

Shift gears often.

When biking, wear a helmet.

Be kind to animals.

Adopt a pet.

Be kind to children.

Adopt a child.

Support charities as you can.

Visit a new place once a week.

Lay down on the floor at least once a day.

Use more bicarbonate of soda.

Use more vinegar.

Reject most TV.

Reject most movies.

Read a book.

Then read another book.

Then tell someone about the first book.

Join a club.

Vote.

Make love as much as possible.

Hug your kids.

Listen to as many people as possible.

Look people in the eyes

Above all,

Be well..

54

The Courage to Be

Tuesday, March 7, 2006

This morning, I read with great sadness of the death of Dana Reeve. This woman was a great bodhisattva. Her memory, like that of her husband, will be a blessing for us all.

It is not difficult to find models for us to live by. Dana and Christopher Reeve were such models. Then so is a small one named Jennifer I saw on Discovery Health Channel the other day who was born without a face and endures tremendous pain and suffering as she undergoes a countless series of surgeries to build her a face. Then there is her family, and the doctors and nurses, her extended family, neighbors and friends. When one tosses a pebble into the pond where do the ripples cease?

Dana Reeve was only 44 years old. She had never smoked a cigarette. Yet one in five women contract lung cancer who have never smoked in their lives. One wonders. These are people who led their lives fully. They developed great courage and compassion. They suffered, but they also succeeded.

When we live our lives in this way, directly, being with each event, each feeling that arises and still maintain our balance and our determination to be of service in the world, we are living buddhas.

I saw video of little Jennifer shortly after a massive surgery, pick up a striker and play with toy bells. The sound of the bell is both a call to mindfulness and a reminder that there is always joy in our lives even in the midst of great pain should we choose to experience it.

55

What it is

Friday, March 10, 2006

When we are being in the present moment, as it is, there is no room for anything else. This moment, as it is, is full and complete. So, what is this moment, as it is?

Sitting Zazen without sitting Zazen. Cleaning without cleaning. Talking without talking. Eating without eating. Listening without listening.

Zen is being complete in this moment without adding words, names, labels, judgements, thoughts, likes or dislikes to it.

When we are correctly oriented to living this way, everything becomes easy. No problem.

Living this way allows our breathing to be what it is: free.
Living this way allows our Buddha-nature to flower.
Living this way allows our love to be itself.
Living this way allows our compassion to enfold the planet.
Living this way allows all things to be One.

56

Dealing with the News

Saturday, March 11, 2006

On my Yahoo 360 blog I have been recounting the Ten Grave Precepts. Today's precept is the fifth which asks us not to cloud our minds. Usually this is taken to mean not to drink to the point of not being sober. It is also an invitation not to ingest drugs or other toxins that will injure us or otherwise cause harm. Thich Nhat Hahn, the Vietnamese Buddhist Monk and Peace Worker has suggested that this precept includes taking things into us such as images or information which will poison us. Poison us with greed, hatred, and delusion.

This morning's news included a piece on the killing of Mr. Tom Fox, a Quaker and a Christian Peace Worker in Iraq who was taken hostage. Reports are that he was beaten, cut, and then shot in the chest and the head. Bound, his body was dumped on the street.

There are several "Friends" on this list. My deepest condolences to you.

My sense is that to avoid news can be harmful, as harmful as hiding one's head in the sand. The problem isn't the news or the images, but in what we do with them. If the images and the news causes hatred and anger, big problem. If, on the other hand, the information invites us to examine ourselves, our feelings, our relationships, our own actions, and thereby causes us to stand upright in the face of these three poisons, then we are being bodhisattvas.

The Buddha invited us to sit in a graveyard and be with a decomposing body. The image, the scent, the processes of decomposition are all "poisons" to those who seek nothing but the flowers of life. Yet all flowers eventually lose their bloom, wilt, keel over, wrinkle up and die. They then become part of the environment, enriching it with nutrients for the next seed beginning to grow.

When we stand apart from the natural cycles of living and dying, loving and hating, we are not able to help, we lose touch, live in a fantasy, and become incapable of connecting to others.

So, we should sit with this atrocity. We should invite our feelings to enter us, process them as we would the presence of a decomposing body in our living room. Turn away the eyes and you become salt. Care for the body and you become a bodhisattva.

It is most challenging work.

57

Interconnection

Sunday, March 12, 2006

As the sun rises and warms the desert, I am sipping hot green tea at the computer. My heart is still and I am opening my eyes to see you. We are each a part of this wonderful universe. Each necessary. Each vital. The universe cannot exist without us. As each thing has its causes and conditions, each thing is deeply interwoven in the fabric of space and time. Where does one begin and end? Truely? Seeds from parents are planted and arise producing seeds that are planted and arise and so on and so on. Small changes here and there, divergence, complexity, life.

So, as I type here and am aware of the keys touching electrical pads, sending pulses out through fiber optic cables, patterns abound, connect with other patterns, and there we are: a universe. We are one, here and now. As you read. As I move on through my day, and you yours. My message is with you and you are with me. We are together. A good thing.

If we live this way, how difficult to injure each other! How difficult to willingly cause harm! Be peace today. Be yourself.

58

Leaving Home

Monday, March 13, 2006

This morning there are clouds in the sky over the desert. Yesterday was another windy day. My hope is that this afternoon will be beautiful and sunny with a clear sky, but if it isn't, well it will be beautiful as it is and I will appreciate it.

Each day offers itself to us as a partner in our experience in this process of life. Our practice is to be open to this process and receive its teachings.

What does this really mean?

Partly it is about leaving home. This means leaving what we believe we know at our bed as we rise and enter the day. If we go through our day knowing then what are we learning? What sort of room is there in our heads for something new and different?

Leaving home is scary. It requires courage and faith. Courage to face things without a shield, faith that what we receive will not harm us.

We are life's students. Adult learners who have immense capacity for both enlightenment and delusion. One requires a shedding of self, the other grasps the self. When we shed our self: our assumptions, our beliefs, even our self-proclaimed values, we are truly open to learning by direct experience.

So, today, please practice this sort of openness. Have faith that the process is what it is and in the end, you are one with it. Have courage to be there, present in each moment. A buddha.

59

Encouraging Zazen

Wednesday, March 15, 2006

Zazen can be the foundation of our life. When we make it so, it is the ground we walk on, the support we have through the day, our greatest teacher, our stalwart companion. . What is it about this practice that makes it so?

Deciding to take a seat, gather oneself together, enfold one's hands to complete a circle, and place our attention on witnessing only, enables us.

It enables us to settle down. It enables us to pay attention to the inner workings of our lives. It enables us to see the interaction between the inner and outer workings of the universe. All without having to do anything about anything.

Over time a certain deep and abiding trust develops from this practice. A trust in the universal processes of living and dying. We learn that we can let go and everything will still exist. Me and you cease to have real meaning. We see that we create meaning, and in so doing we create our suffering.

All of these rise and fall in our awareness, and still, we don't engage them. Our job is to simply witness.

I encourage each of you to take up this practice. Make this practice a model for living.

Any moment will do. Just pay attention. At some point, decide to sit more formally. Find a time, find a place. Sit down and practice Zazen. In that moment, know that peace is not only possible, but a reality.

60

Peace

Thursday, March 16, 2006

Peace does not come without effort. Peace is an active process. We must deliberately put down arms, we must deliberately attempt to find other ways to solve conflicts, address grievances, and correct wrongs. Adding violence just adds violence. It resolves nothing. Our government will continue to misbehave until we make it unacceptable by moral authority, electoral process, public opinion, and the weight of our votes.

I am not naive. I do not believe standing around on a corner will stop a war. But what I do believe is that standing around on a corner with simple signs of conscience will begin to create conditions for alternative views in people. We must stand as witnesses. The majority must not be silent. Everyday soldiers and civilians in the war-torn parts of this world are suffering and dying without a voice saying enough. We can stand for an hour as a voice to help in some small way bring them home. And if we don't have the time, there is something clearly wrong with our priorities.

61

One Way or the Other?

Friday, March 17, 2006

Jeff, a faithful reader of my blog, quotes Warner-sensei and asks a question:

Society is offering us two options both of which are completely wrong. The hawks are wrong and the doves are wrong because both sides only want to see more conflict, more wars, more suffering. What's wrong with the hawks is far too clear to bother stating. But the doves cannot be happy unless there are hawks for them to fight against. The "peace movement" is only happy when there are wars to protest. They don't have the slightest interest in peace. ~ Brad Warner

So, do you understand what he is talking about here? I'm not sure I get it..

———

Warner-sensei is pointing out a deep truth here in a way common among classical Zen Teachers. The truth is in neither one position or another, but in the fact that suffering arises when we cling to one position or another. True happiness comes when we cease seeking and begin experiencing. This is why we should not "fight" against war, poverty, racism or any other injustice. Our practice is to be.

When we are peace, compassion, wisdom, with no "I" involved, then what? No struggle. Zen Buddhism, in the "engaged" sense, is just so. We don't say we do, we do. We don't fight, we become. We are witnesses and participants in the world. We witness violence and participate in peace.

All of the true non-violence teachers understand this: do not strike back, yet do not yield in the heart/mind. Our bodies will break, as Gandhi points out, and they will have our broken bodies, but they will not have us.

Conflicts in absolutes are always understood by seeing the absolutes as relative.

62

Three Years

Saturday, March 18, 2006

Please take a few minutes today and consider peace. This is the third anniversary of our invasion of Iraq. Peace happens when we become peace. To become peace means to become complete within ourselves and others. Our practice, Zazen, Kinhin, Samu, Oryoki: all are peacemaking practices. They are practices that teach us serenity in a flood of world activity.

When we sit, we sit. When we walk, we walk. When we work, we work. When we eat, we eat. Nothing special. Nothing added. We are serene reflection in motion.

To be at war is to be at conflict and to be angry, greedy, and deluded. Who wishes to walk that path?

Today, please take a small sign that simply reads "Peace." Go outside and stand.

63

Good Night and Good Luck

Sunday, March 19, 2006

Yesterday we watched "Good Night and Good Luck" a film about Edward R. Murrow and the McCarthy era in the United States. It was well worth watching and I am glad we bought it so we can watch it again a few times over. George Clooney did a wonderful job. It is an eloquent film.

The film is quite a reminder of things. A reminder that fear can drive us to the brink of willingly giving up our freedoms and responsibilities in order to feel safe. A reminder that such fear can be very easily exploited. And a reminder that keeping vigilant and courageous has its costs.

Of course, we don't need to be reminded. We are in a similar era. Our fear and safely needs are being exploited on a daily basis. In this din of warnings, people tend to cower, acquiesce to the powers that be in order to be assured of their safety. While safety is not such a bad thing, being safe at the price of freedom is.

We must be diligent in two directions simultaneously. We must be witness to the erosion of our freedoms and to the threat to our lives. Indeed, there are those in this world who would kill us, so afraid they are of change. Yet to become them is not progression but regression. In order to be safe and free, we must be without hindrance.

How to be without hindrance? Practice Zazen.

64

Balancing Act

Tuesday, March 21, 2006

With so much going on outside in the world, it is easy to go there and get lost or caught up in the whirlwind. Our perception is that it is outside of us and is so important that we must do something. War, poverty, injustice, disease; these are awful things worthy of our attention and our energy.

Yet, in truth, these things are not out there, but inside of us. In our minds and our hearts. We respond with a disturbed body, we become ill. In such a condition we are not present for our friends and family. We are not fully there for our co-workers and employers.

These things are important. We should do what we can to ease suffering, stop violence, bring health to the ill. We should do so, however, with a healthy mind, a healthy body, and a wholesome heart. This requires us to establish boundaries, maintain these boundaries, and nurture those boundaries.

A boundary is a point where doing begins to hurt us.

Recognizing that there are limits to our power and capacity to be of service, to absorb suffering, and to be present, is a necessary first step. Willingness to say no is the second step. Finally, we must nurture ourselves as a third step. Eating well, getting enough sleep, getting exercise, practicing

Zazen, opening our hearts to others in discussion: these are ways of taking good care of ourselves.

In the absolute sense we are one with the universe. In the relative sense we are just a finite body with finite energy. Our practice is to live between the two recognizing the truth and needs of both.

65

A Full Cup

Thursday, March 23, 2006

There is a story about a scholar who visits an Old Zen Master to receive instruction. The Master pours tea into a cup for the scholar; full, the cup overflows until the scholar shouts "stop!"

Unless we are willing to empty ourselves of what we think we know, there can be no room for what presents itself in each moment. Zazen is like a slow leak.

Take your cup and go.

66

Being a Buddha

Friday, March 24, 2006

When we sit Zazen we gather ourselves together, fold our legs, and sit down. Our breath comes together with our mind, our skin, eyes, ears, nose, and mouth. Mind rises and falls, dances a fast dance, then slow dance, sometimes no dance. There comes a moment of integration. Stillness. Once again things begin to stir, once more thought, once more feeling, taste, touch, and sound. Stillness, motion, no difference, no preference. When sitting, just sit.

This practice enables us to see clearly how we are buddhas in each moment. The moment we set aside our preferences, navigate according to our precepts, manifest the perfections, we are buddhas. This is so in the middle of choppy waters and calm waters; in the middle of stinking garbage and wonderful roses; when we are suffering and not suffering. Buddha means awake. Nothing more or less. Awake.

Living awake changes everything and changes nothing. Living awake means coffee is both coffee and not-coffee at the same time, no difference. Concept and experience clearly seen as separate and the same. So difficult, so easy.

I invite you to engage yourself in this practice. Sit. Gather yourself. Awaken. Move on.

67

Being Present

Tuesday, March 28, 2006

To be alive means to feel. Sometimes we feel good, sometimes not. Sometimes we are happy, sometimes not. To be awake means that when we are hot, we are fully hot; when we are cold, we are fully cold. Enlightenment does nothing to make what is there better. It is what we call being one with the universe and the universe is a vast container. Being one with being sick means fully being sick, present with our sickness, completely. A thought of escaping our sickness leads us to suffering as it adds duality to our consciousness, separating us from ourselves, adding a discernment.

When someone we care for is suffering, we suffer. When we are hot, we are hot. When we are cold, we are cold. As we are these things, we naturally do what we can within them. We care for our suffering. We add a blanket, take off a blanket, but we do so without the effort of mental anguish.

The ability to do this comes with the wisdom of mindful presence.

68

Living

Thursday, March 30, 2006

In Zen we aspire to leave no trace. That is, to live without self-interest. How do we attain this? We behave for the benefit of others. And if we are acting for others fully and completely then there is no room for anything else.

The value that we place on ourselves should only be the value needed to sustain us for our work. We eat so that we may benefit others. We practice Zazen so that we might benefit others. We clothe ourselves to benefit others. We are in relationship to benefit others. With this right understanding, all other paths of the Noble way unfold with ease and genuineness.

In the absence of self, what is there? Compassion. Our practice is to make compassion a living manifestation in the universe. We do this through continuous, moment-to-moment generosity, morality, patience, diligence, meditation, and wisdom.

We realize that we are the other shore and that we attained the other shore and that we have never left.

69

Zen is Work

Saturday, April 1, 2006

Being a Zen Buddhist is much more than words and a good feeling, more than hours on a cushion staring at a wall, more than vows and commitments to some ideal. Zen is work.

Rise in the morning with an intent to see clearly, to help every being. Eat with awareness of all of the lives and hands that went into bringing your food to you. Breathe with awareness, walk with awareness. Feel with awareness. Work with awareness.

Awareness is what? Of everything: the air, the scent in the air, the feel, the sound, the thought, the taste of life lived in interdependence with the universe. This is true 'multi-tasking.'

We see a hungry person, we offer them food. No question. We see thoughtlessness, we correct it. We see injury, we help nurse it. We see fighting, we help stop it.

We don't just say, "I believe!" and go on being a jerk, thinking our belief will save us. Belief of this sort is for cowards and dilettantes. Living in a world-in-wait for somebody else to make everything right.

Zen Buddhists do.

70

In Motion

Sunday, April 2, 2006

This morning is overcast and drizzling. The rain is wonderful. The air is cool and heavy, unlike the desert. Green is unfolding all around. I saw beautiful flowers in bloom this morning. Lots of early birds getting their worms, as well. Life is a good thing when kept in perspective.

I urge each of us to get outside today. Enjoy the weather, whatever it is. It is always a good idea to go outside. It gives us perspective. Sitting on grass. A park bench. Or just walking along and listening, smelling, feeling, that life around us. After a short time, whatever heaviness that we might be bearing, lifts.

We breathe in, knowing we are breathing in, we breathe out, knowing we are breathing out. Short step, long step, jog, walk, run, skip: no matter, we are Zen in motion.

Be well.

71

The Present Moment

Wednesday, April 5, 2006

There was once a monk named Tanzan. Tanzan was an older monk and did not pay close attention to the rules. He ate when he was hungry, slept when he was sleepy. He drank wine on occasion even though intoxicants were forbidden.

One day Tanzan and another monk were walking along and they arrived at a stream. There was a young woman at the stream trying to cross without muddying herself. Tanzan simply picked her up and carried her across the stream, placing her back on the ground, he put his palms together, bowed and continued on his way. Sometime later, Tanzan's companion criticized Tanzan for having touched the young woman by carrying her across the stream. Tanzan simply said to his younger brother, "I put her down miles ago, why is it you still carry her with you?"

Each of us has an opportunity each moment to renew ourselves. Carrying the burdens of the past prevents this. In each moment, be a buddha. When you are angry, be angry and let it go. When you are sad, be sad and let it go. When you are happy, be happy and let it go. To experience life fully and completely is being a buddha. To live in the past or in worry or anticipation of the future is to be asleep.

72

Love and Hate

Thursday, April 6, 2006

There is a lingering coolness, fresh and crisp, in the air this morning at my window as I type. Although the desert sun is rising and quickly warming the air, it is still a delicious taste of spring. It is important to experience directly. Feel the air. Smell the plants. Taste the interior of your mouth in the morning. It is important to do so without commenting mentally about the experiences. It is the commentary that takes us away from the truth. Within split seconds we are in the mental world of ideas, likes, dislikes; the world of labels and categories. While this world has its place and its function, it is a world that separates us from ourselves, internally and externally.

The Buddha taught that hate produces hate. He taught that love produces love. He also taught, more deeply, that both hate and love are part of the same thing, that we and the world, the entire universe are one. In this teaching if we attain it, we see that to hate another is to hate ourselves. To love another is to love ourselves. We see in this that every moment, every gesture, is a universal one.

Living in a dualistic world, we create groups of assumptions in our mind/body. We gather experiences, words, feelings, sensations and store them in our consciousness. This store becomes a toxic filter through which we push our each experience through. This is like that, we say, and respond accordingly. What is missed in this process is the fact that this is not that, this is this! Itself.

In our response, we gather steam, we justify ourselves, well these people act like this, they speak such and such, they must be this or that. The response re-enforces the initial belief and that re-enforcement is stored in our consciousness.

On a particular blog I have been engaging in a set of discussions that have demonstrated this and drove the point home to me in no uncertain terms. The people on this blog site see me as critical, hateful, and unpriestly. I agree. I have spoken within my store of experience, allowing it to distort my perception and not see them for themselves, but rather my creation of them. This creation and my response to it has been poisonous. Polarization is easy, understanding is challenging. Hate is easy, love is challenging. It is very easy to live in a thought world, a world of preconception, distortion, prejudice. It is a whole other matter to relinquish the baggage, as Tanzan, (in my blog note yesterday) and stand directly and openly, doing what the situation actually calls for.

May we each work hard to live directly and with deep compassion for our neighbors and for the strangers among us. We are all we have, you know. It would be wise to nurture this most precious resource.

73

Sesshin

Friday, April 7, 2006

We begin our Hannamatsuri Sesshin this evening at the Refuge in the mountains. We gather ourselves to sit in meditation in order to both relieve suffering and prepare ourselves to relieve suffering. In this period we recall the birth of the Buddha, honoring this man with sweet tea and flowers. We will sit for the next few days, eat in mindful silence, work in mindful silence, and practice deeply together the six paramitas of generosity, morality, patience, diligence, meditation, and wisdom.

Our Zen Center practices extended periods of Zazen monthly as a day of mindfulness (Zazenkai) and quarterly as weekend Sesshin. During these periods we practice as monastics with a long sitting schedule, periods of samu (work meditation) and study periods. The time is spent in mindful silence with a minimum of verbal interaction. The purpose is to deliberately slow down both mind and body, cast our senses inward, and develop and deepen our personal awareness to the extent that, paradoxically, this "self" drops away.

As this happens, our true, compassionate nature is given an opportunity to bloom. During this time, my hope is that each of you will practice in some way with us, that you may each be part of the eternal garden of life.

74

Life of Fiction

Sunday, April 9, 2006

In the world of the everyday, we are prone to easily lose our grip. We think constantly, telling ourselves all sorts of things, creating worlds upon worlds of thoughts and feelings about the ideas we create. At some point we need to clearly understand that this world we create is not real, but rather, a fiction. It is a mental construction and truly means nothing. In fact it can become a hindrance to our life.

When we are living in the fictional world of our thoughts, ideas, and feelings, we are not experiencing our true, actual lives. When we live in a "belief system" that system organizes, colors, and frames our experience. This is not actual experience, this is filtered and distorted thought-as-experience.

How can we truly appreciate our life when we are so busy thinking about it?

When practicing Zazen we are experiencing our self. There is no other self. Just this self, just this moment. All moments past are seen as thoughts in motion. All moments future are thoughts in motion. Zazen clarifies. When we are on the cushion, present in the here and now, witnessing our actual self as it is, then we are Buddha.

Do we need to give up our goals? Do we need to stop thinking?

No! Of course not. What this means is that we practice to see clearly what is what. That is, what is in relation to what? Thoughts are thoughts, that is all. Goals are thoughts made into objectives with a plan to attain them, but they remain mental constructs. We suffer in direct relation to how closely we hold them and how we use them. If we hold them close, are highly invested in them, use them as some sort of litmus test for ourselves to assess our value, then we are giving them far too much power and are, in effect, using them to eclipse our actual, real life in the here and now. We do not need to supplant our actual life with thoughts and beliefs, living in hopes and dreams. We can live in this life, with this self, as it is, and appreciate it for the blessing that it is. We do this when we make sure we are our lives and not our mental constructs. Another way of saying this is to live deliberately with open eyes.

75

Doing and Not Doing

Monday, April 10, 2006

Is there time in your day for yourself? A moment where you can stop and be still, opening yourself to everything by not doing?

If we do not create such time and opportunity, we waste away. Living well requires both motion and stillness, doing and non-doing. If we tend to a plant too much it will die. If we tend to it too little, it will also die. We are the same.

How much of each is sufficient? In human terms, what is tending and non-tending?

Very excellent questions. Questions that are for your practice of living your life.

The most important thing is to both answer them, then practice!

Life is short, you have a precious opportunity, get going!

76

Is everyone eating leftovers?

Tuesday, April 11, 2006

Master Dogen writes:

The ordinary states, the outer ordinary states --- bamboo in the mountains, cypresses in the yard. Partial sage, ultimate sage --- spring flowers, autumn moon.

When you have attained the realm of Zen, there is no Zen; when you clarify the realm of desire, there is no desire.

There is no one in the whole world who understands Buddhism --- everyone is eating leftovers.

To say it is like something would miss it --- it is not in the company of myriad things. What stages are there? What do you want with the beyond?

Eihei Koroku (translated by Cleary)

Our practice of the Buddha Way is our practice of the Buddha way. Yours is not mine. Each of us must enter the gate ourselves. My words to you are like shit. They mean little to nothing, mere tracks of one who has gone before.

When we experience the wind in our face, the shock of a sound, or the smell of a corpse or flower, we are experiencing ourselves. As I paint a picture, it is just a painting of a picture. Quite different from your actual experience.

I urge you to practice the Buddha Way for yourself. What does this mean? Nothing really. Just stop and sit still. Create an opportunity for you to experience the universe as it is, rather than as you think it is.

77

Self and the Relativity of Truth

Wednesday, April 12, 2006

On my Yahoo 360 blogsite, there is a place called a "Blast." It enables the blogger to make a quick little statement, ask a question, etc. Every morning I create a new "Blast" statement and change the color theme of the blog. I feel this keeps things fresh and present.

This morning's blast thought was about individuality. When we allow our identification with "self" to fall away, then all sorts of things are made possible. Dogen suggests that everything becomes our Teacher. This is so because we have no self-acting as a hindrance. It goes deeper than that, however.

When we cease identifying with this "self" and this "body" then death and life themselves cease to carry weight. We can become aware of the great stream of living and dying, like the ocean's tide, eternally flowing.

More, with no individual self, everything can be more clearly understood in its relation to everything else: a great web or net containing both point and interconnection.

To say we cease identifying with self does not mean self does not exist. It means self is understood in its proper relation to the universe. In this sense we begin to identify with the great vastness, understanding the relativity of all things.

It is in this understanding that we begin to see truth as both relative and absolute simultaneously.

78

Evaluation of Soto Zen : a response

Friday, April 14, 2006

Original message by Guy:

Good day all sangha, I've been exploring the Soto line of Zen for the past year and have started to come to conclusions that may draw me away from it.

So let me see if my understanding is correct.

It seems to me that Soto's view is that if there is something wrong with reality, what is wrong is not reality. We are already perfectly awakened; there is nothing to achieve. And I fully agree with this, to a point. The point is this. Isn't the act of "just sitting", although not trying to achieve anything, doing exactly that? It's clearing the mirror of our minds.

If we were perfectly awake, we wouldn't clear anything from our minds when we meditate. So there is something wrong, we live in Samsara. Our view is not perfect, although buddha said it is possible to achieve.

In one of So Daiho's post the other day he made reference to Dogen's statement that we are all living on leftovers. Sidhartha found the way, we just follow what he did. So i consider this the source to fall back on even though the cannons were not written in buddha's time. Brings me to two conclusions. First, suffering exist, and Buddha advocated alleviating suffering. Seems to acknowledge that something might just be wrong.

Second, buddha taught in ways other than just meditation. After recently being admonished by a Soto priest for saying to face one's fears; he came back and reinforced my point by saying that Buddha sent his monks to sleep with corpses. Hard to say what Buddha was trying to say here: maybe it was confronting the fear of death, maybe he was telling his monks they smell bad. But it points to teaching off the mat. So maybe there is more than "just sitting".

Anyway, this is my conflict with Soto. Anybody able to resolve this?

In gassho

Guy has written an excellent post above. He asks similar questions Master Dogen asked many centuries ago. Let me try to walk through this as a morning message.

We are indeed, enlightened and perfect as we are. Why practice? Dogen asked this very question. Because we possess Buddha nature does not mean we arer in touch with it. Because we can run or walk or talk, does not mean we can do it without practice. We inherently possess, but we must manifest.

The Sixth Patriarch uses a similar metaphor in his Platform Sutra. A rival for the robe suggests the mind is like a mirror and that practice must be used to clear the dust from its surface. Hui-Neng argues back:

> *Bodhi originally has no tree,*
> *The mirror also has no stand.*
> *Buddha nature is always clean and pure;*
> *Where is there room for dust?*

> *(Yoplansky translation, p. 132)*

The questions raised in this post are essential. They go to the heart of the matter. What is "reality?" Why do we even concern ourselves with it? What is "enlightenment?" What is "Samsara?" What is "dust, the mirror?" If A is A, why B?

These questions are not an evaluation of Soto. They are the questions that take us to the cushion. They are the questions that provide a 'platform' for our existence and thus, our practice.

Apparent contradiction and paradox in Zen should always be understood as existing within a certain point of reference: relative truth. Resolution of the paradox exists in Absolute truth. Practice teaches us both the difference and the means of being simultaneously in both. Samsara/Nirvana: heads/tails, one coin.

There are many practice gates. Zazen is the first and last, but this is Zazen properly understood. What is this "properly understood?" That is your practice.

If we sit with a corpse in a cemetery, as once was done, we do not stink, we discover stink and the sweet smell of a rose are essentially the same. Our valuations are something we add. If we sit with a corpse and witness decomposition, we see life. We see process. We see ourselves as something not dependent on form. Such activities as sitting with corpses, sitting with ourselves, eating in mindful silence, tea ceremonies, koans, the smack of the kyosaku on our shoulders are simply means, but here's the thing. They are also ends. Reality is 'perfect' as it can be no other way than it is. Our thoughts about it, how we discern it, our relative comfort and discomfort within it, these are imperfection.

I hope this short answer helps.

79

Being One

Saturday, April 15, 2006

We have been exploring reality from the point of view that both objective and subjective experience are one. One makes the other, the other makes the one. In fact, they are the same reality experienced in different ways, from different perspectives: very functional. We must be able to see subject and object at certain times, use thought to plan, etc. But we must also not lose sight of the fact that this is an artificial device created through the way our brain works in order to enhance our survival. Reality itself, is not two, but one.

When we approach our life, our practice, in this way, we begin to see that everything is sacred, nothing is profane. Indeed, such categories are local devices, rather than universal truth. As we light a stick of incense, all beings are lighting a stick of incense. As we bow, all beings are bowing. As we bring ourselves to the other shore, all beings are brought to the other shore. You and God share the same space, the same reality. When you touch, God touches. When you see, God sees. When you eat, God eats. Being one with God changes everything.

This is nothing more than the simple truth.

So difficult, however, to realize, so powerful the discriminating brain.

Whether we each believe in God is irrelevant. Call God the universe, it doesn't really matter. What matters is your willingness to open yourself to its vastness.

80

A Seasonal Message

Sunday, April 16, 2006

We have an opportunity today to be reminded of the blessings of the yearly cycle. This is spring, Easter, Passover, Hannamatsuri, a time of hope and re-generation. Many cultures come out of an agrarian background. Life cycles were closely connected to our planet's seasonal cycles. In this modern era, we seem to have lost that connection on many levels, As a result of this disconnect, some of the real meanings of the season are lost to us. To compensate we fall back on belief. Belief is a wonderful thing, in some ways, a hindrance in others.

When living in belief, we live in the world of the mind. Hopeful, we are looking for tomorrow, not living in the experience of this moment. This is why, in some sense, Zen sees hope as a problem. Hope takes us away from the work at hand, though it also can inspire us and motivate us to move into the future.

As in all things, a balance is very important.

For those who are Christian on the list, Happy Easter! For those Jewish, Happy Pesach, for those who are singularly Buddhist, a joyous Hannamatsuri.

May we all be happy and present.

81

Zazen

Monday, April 17, 2006

When practicing Zazen we should be present with ourselves and our environment, experiencing without thinking, feelings, tasting, smelling or touching. As we sit, our mind speaks to us, sometimes through thought, sometimes through sensation. We feel an itch, or something crawling, or a twitch, a stitch. We think. We see our thoughts. We might smell something, hear something, taste something. What is it?

This question arises and if we are not very careful, we are exploring it. Big mistake. Our Zazen is not to explore the interior and exterior of our minds and bodies. Our Zazen is to simply practice serene reflection: presence without attachment/.

Shikantaza is the practice of wholeheartedly hitting the mark while seated. What is the mark? What is this present moment, exactly, before a thought or perception arises? That is the mark.

82

Bodhidharma's Wake Up Sermon

Tuesday, April 18, 2006

From the First Patriarch, Bodhidharma, in his Wake-Up Sermon (translated by Red Pine) Bodhidharma, founder of Zen, was born in the year 440. He came to China late in the fifth century of the common era.

"Whoever knows that the mind is a fiction and devoid of anything real knows that his own mind neither exists nor doesn't exist. Mortals keep creating the mind, claiming that it exists. And arhats keep negating the mind, claiming it doesn't exist. But bodhisattvas and buddhas neither create nor negate the mind. This is what is meant by the mind that neither exists nor doesn't exist. The mind that neither exists nor doesn't exist is called the Middle Way." (p. 53)

This is a profoundly deep teaching. It at once delineates between an awakened person and a non awakened person but goes beyond that to suggest that an awakened person must go past awakening to become a bodhisattva and a buddha. By a "mortal" Bodhidharma is referring to a ordinary person living in an ordinary life, unaware of his original nature. This is a sleeping person, a person on autopilot, going through the motions of living, but completely not present.

An awakened person, an arhat, is one who has attained awakening. This person's eyes are opened to the true nature of things. Self is extinguished, impermanence understood, and emptiness attained. Yet this is not enough. Buddha was fully awakened, but he got up from his cushion and entered the world. He taught. He healed. He sat with every sort of person from pauper to king. He made a difference in the world through his work.

When we realize that subject and object have relational existence, that one is and is not at the same time, and that we are able to live within the vast and eternal processes of life, then we are both buddhas and bodhisattvas. Buddhas because we have realized and attained this highest teaching, bodhisattvas because we set our "selves" aside to be in service to the entire universe throughout time.

One who attains this understanding recognizes there is no past, present or future; no you, no me, no subject, no object; yet lives at the same moment within time, subject and object, and does so without thought as hindrance.

83

Another Day

Wednesday, April 19, 2006

Rev. Gozen, my disciple and abbot of the Zen Center of Las Cruces, gave a wonderful talk this evening. He spoke of the moment before the word. We are so caught in words and ideas that we fail to really see. When we see with words and ideas, we aren't seeing reality. I sat in silence there with him in the Zendo feeling a number of things. I was listening intently and the Dharma was alive and present in the room with us. The tea was excellent. Ryan did a good job as both Ino and server of the tea. I made some mental notes to assist him in the future.

A small Zen Center is an intimate place. We sit in rows facing the great white wall, the scent of sandalwood incense slips to and fro, and the soft flicker of the candle is just enough light to feel warmed by its presence. Our bell is large and sits on a wonderful cushion. I remember finding it in a shop in San Francisco one day while attending a retreat with the Dalai Lama. On that journey I also found our Buddha statue and incense holder.

It is quite a task to establish a new Zen Center. Many small details. But the hearts beat and the many hands come together; soon we are there, sitting silently in rows supporting each other as we practice our Way.

So, this morning began with a lot of energy. My wife was to read her poetry at a local writer's group. I went with her. Her work, whimsical word portraits of our grandchildren, was warmly received. Lunch with friends at a restaurant where I happened to met a couple I married some time ago. Things between them are going well. I am happy for them. I drove Judy home, then went grocery shopping. After putting away the groceries, I rode my bike to the weekly peace vigil where I pulled my sign out of my backpack and stood for an hour in the afternoon sun. There were so many horns honking in support! Then the long ride home. A nice salad for dinner and a shower. Time to go to the Zen Center for Zazen.

Tonight, I am here with you. Writing and offering some small voice. Tomorrow morning a walk in the desert, a meeting with the rabbi, a speedwork session and a weight workout. Life is good.

84

A Blackened Nose

Thursday, April 20, 2006

There was once a nun who carried a gold leafed Buddha everywhere she wandered. She would light her incense offering each day, but did not wish to share it, so she created a device which kept the incense from moving about, instead it was funneled into the Buddha's nose. Over time, the gold leafed Buddha became particularly ugly with a blackened nose.

When we practice our lives, we are practicing for all beings, not for Buddhas and ourselves. Our practice should be for the benefit of others. To practice otherwise is not the Buddha Way.

So, when we eat, we eat for all beings, recognizing the many lives that went into the food before us, the sharing of so many hands in creating it and bringing it to us. When we drink, we drink with all beings, refreshing ourselves, and thereby all others. When we work, we work for the benefit of all beings, and when we sleep, we sleep with all beings restoring our bodies, rebuilding muscle, resting our minds, and soothing our hearts.

When we live this way, there is no self. Just living this way. Attempting to keep life for ourselves blackens our nose.

85

Reality

Friday, April 21, 2006

From Cheng Li's Tales of Kwan Yin

Adapted by a friend from a translation by John Blofield

Transcendence
Now I have done with Su-tras
and pious practices.
Day and night I recite the Bo-dhi-sat-tva's sacred name,
rejoicing in the beauty of it's sound.
NOT for me it's recitation in multiples of One-hundred and Eight,
as though it were a duty.
Does the runner count his breaths, the poet his words,
or the stream it's ripples?
You sentient beings who seek deliverance,
why do you NOT let go?
When sad,
Let go of the cause of sadness.
When wrathful,
Let go of the occasion of wrath.
When covetous or lustful,
Let go of the object of desire.

From moment to moment,
be free from grasping
at the illusion of a permanent
or separate "self."

Where there is
NO separate "self" to grasp,
there can be NO permanent sorrow,
NO graspable desire;
NO causally-separate "me" to weep,
NO compositionally-separate "me" to lust,
NO circumstantially-separate "being" to die
and NO perceptually-separate "being" to be reborn.
The winds of circumstance
blow across the infinite expanse
of NON-graspable emptiness.
Whom can they harm?

This is the essence of the source of compassion. In the Heart Sutra we chant "No hindrance in the mind, therefore no fear." Once we are able to see through to the other side, be the other side, having never left; that is, realize this side and that side (birth and death, heaven and hell, samsara and nirvana, God and Me) are the same, two sides of the same coin, then there is no hindrance, nothing to fear, no self to be harmed. Nothing left but the vast processes of the universe and our vast compassion within them.

We establish our reality through our perceptions and these perceptions flow through our senses. While "objective reality" exists without our presence, it depends upon our perceptions of it for its definition in human terms. So, no human contact, no definition. Some may say, then, no existence.

In this we must ask what is existence? What does it mean to be real? Does the tree falling in the forest make a sound? What is tree? Forest? Falling" Sound? Are these all not human concepts? No human, no human conceptualization, then?

Zazen.

86

God

Saturday, April 22, 2006

Do not trust your point of view, it is as shaky as you are. Our points of view are all relative to our senses and the clarity with which they perceive. Even with the clearest perception, the result is a few chemical reactions in our brains which create a picture for us to see. A point of view is just that. It is not the thing itself.

What is the thing itself? In Zen Buddhism we call it suchness. That which is before perception. It has no name, desires no name. It is vast emptiness manifest. Emptiness refers to lack of substance, lack of permanence. Some might "name" this "God."

Names are odd, really. They tend to be nouns in the English language. As such they can be very misleading. We often think because we name something, we either understand it or control it. This is one of the psychological truths of biblical times. God tells Adam to go out and name all of the animals, suggesting that he will then have dominion over them. Today, in many forms of psychotherapy, naming a problem is a tool employed to enable the patient to feel some control in their lives over against a problem. Yet these are devices only. Tools of the trade, really. And they have limited value.

At some point in our spiritual development, such devices not only lose their value but become actual hindrances to our growth. To understand God as a noun is to miss His true existence entirely. To understand God as a verb also misses the mark. So if not a noun and not a verb, then what? God and Vast Emptiness are beyond our ability to name them.

Here's the thing: there is no place where God is not. When we attain this then we see clearly. There is no thing that God is not. There is no voice that is not God. Not one place where God is not.

In Zen Buddhism, we practice to realize such things, regardless of whether or not we are theists. The reality of God is not important. In whatever His form, He is, or is not. Like the universe itself, we can take His existence for granted or not, it changes nothing except in ourselves. Call it universe, call it God, but appreciate it fully.

To understand ourselves as human beings misses the mark completely, as well. We too are works in progress. Not nouns, not verbs. In both cases we are left in boxes with tight lids on top.

The point of Zazen is to blow the lid off. Blow the lid off until we realize there is no box, nor a lid to blow, nor a blowing itself. There is just this.

It is *this* that is *suchness*.

87

The Three Pure Precepts

Sunday, April 23, 2006

This afternoon I would like to talk to you about the Three Pure Precepts. These are the first precepts after the Three Refuges in the list of Sixteen Bodhisattva Vows. The Three Pure Precepts are as follows: Cease doing evil; Do good; Do good for all beings.

To cease doing evil is really simple. One just stops doing bad stuff. What bad stuff, you ask? Anything that harms another being. Within this precept are all the others. Ahimsa, that old Hindu concept of non-harming is at the source. If we at least do not harm, we are doing well.

Second, a positive precept, do good. What good? Anything that will be good to do. Good and bad do not exist independently of our behavior. We must bring good into the world, just as we cease bringing bad into the world. All it takes is a willingness to be present and do what is necessary.

Third, bring about good for all beings, now this one is a challenge. It's a call to social action, like the Jewish concept of T'zadikah or Christian charity. We are not isolated beings, living on islands apart from each other. We are on a planet where the whole eco-system is interdependent on us. We should care for all beings, nurture all beings, be well in a world of pain and suffering and bring a relief to as much suffering as we can. This is a challenge for most of us as we tend to live as if we are in bubbles. As we all know, however, bubbles are quite delicate and are easily popped. None of us can afford social isolation anymore.

One need not be a Zen Buddhist to do these things. One simply needs to be willing to care.

88

The Present Moment

Tuesday, April 25, 2006

Typically, I sit half lotus with left ankle on right thigh. My body has accommodated this stable position and I settle into it easily. Such habits are not good and we should arouse ourselves from them. This morning, I sat reversing this half lotus and felt my body not settle. This tension assists me in staying in the moment and not falling asleep in the habit of body and mind.

I have talked at some length about birth and death. Coming and going, as it were, the processes of the life cycle of the universe. These are but imaginings. The past, as does the future, do not exist except in the mind's eye. They are chimera and take us away from what is real, this very moment.

Process is a delusion. We only understand it when we take our mind's eye and leap out of the immediate moment as if to say we can thus see a panorama of time. Each moment contains all others, past and future. All birth and death are here right now. Yet how false this is. As each birth and death, each thought coming and going, are fiction.

We live only in the moment and are asleep all other times. This moment presents itself the universe as it is and only can be. A hand goes out, we offer a dollar. A child cries, we offer our breast. We are hungry, we eat, when we are sleepy, we sleep. We do what we do as it is to be done.

In this a community of the moment arises. A faith-based community that assumes we each are present and doing what needs to be done. We call this community sangha. It becomes our ground. Just as the Buddha offers us a way, and the Dharma, a teaching on reality, the Sangha provides the foundation.

89

Defining the Spiritual Situation

Wednesday, April 26, 2006

I beg your indulgence here. I am working out some thoughts.

This morning, I went out for the first time in three days. My Little Honey dropped me off at the Bountiful Bakery where I ate a fruit cup and sipped coffee while the rabbi and I discussed meditation with the group. We then got into a discussion about the Gospel of Judas, God, Jesus and the whole enchilada. Within this discussion the notion of our images of God became noticeable.

Images of God are so interesting to me, as they seem reflections of a person's spiritual presence and growth. If we are interested in people these images become very informative, revealing much of what is underneath the public surface. Those needing punitive images, mean old granddads, in the sky are on one side, those without need for an image at all on the other. Most everyone is somewhere sandwiched in between and the sandwich is, per chance, getting tighter.

Images of God can become in-service to political and societal needs. Fear creates one sort of need, love another, acceptance still another, forgiveness yet another. Depending on our definition of the spiritual situation, God and the image we create for him changes. It is important to see this. As it reveals much about who we are and more importantly still, who we are becoming.

In times of turmoil and uncertainty, human beings want or need a degree of comfort. We have a felt need for control and God becomes the agent we apply to. In times of oppression, God becomes a hero who frees us from our slavery. In times of plenty, we are free to reach for self-actualization and God becomes a partner in the manifestation of this effort.

In today's world, there is a growing conflict between vastly different needs for, and understandings of, God. On the one hand, the sweep of change, rapid information flow, explosive growth of knowledge, fuels tremendous fear on the part of those either disenfranchised by that change or those who are a part of a group being dragged along by the force of such a change. On the other hand, there are those who are leading the change. These are the modernists, the scientists, developers, capitalists, and the highly skilled and trained information specialists.

A question arises in the midst, is there a God unaffected by our needs? Do we matter to God? Is God on the one hand "Wholly Other" or are we infinitely "One with Him"?

Is God an anthropomorphic reflection or a standalone deity? What is the spiritual situation?

When contemplating a circle, one first notices its completeness. Something is "inside", something, "outside." Human beings use images to describe thoughts and feelings, attempting to put into a form an abstraction. Infinite is often understood as a vast unbroken circle. The universe as a large bubble. We use nouns to name, verbs as action words. Names, by definition limit the picture. The Hebrew name for God is not a noun, but a verb phrase, I am that I am, I will be that which I will be. And so on. As with God we soon we ask what is outside of infinity?

Maimonides could only define God by negation, as any attempt to positively assert what God was limited God: a paradoxical statement.

Could it be that God is both subject and object, inside and outside, dependent and independent of human beings? Do we create God and are we at the same time created by God?

Systems theory offers us a way of approaching this question. Systems theory simply allows us to see infinitely, one system in relation to another in relation to another. Some larger, some smaller, but all interconnected and dependent on all others. There is no "largest" system. No "smallest" system. No outside of infinite. Perspective forms definition and definition forms perspective. We are limited only by our willingness and ability to detail and expand the ecosystem.

From a Zen Buddhist perspective, God is or is not, may be or may not be. Like all things, we are because other things are, we are not because other things are not. Causation has no beginning or no end. Such things as beginnings and ends are human inventions created by a limited ability of our mind to grasp infinitude. In this sense, Zen is neutral on the matter of God. It is this very neutrality that makes it possible for a Zen practitioner to become clear on God, so to speak. And perhaps is one reason why so many people come to Zen or other forms of Buddhism as a practice starting point.

When you sit down and consider God, your consideration paints a picture of your needs. Your need-set interacts with others, sometimes in concordance, sometimes in conflict. Regardless of how, the need-set points to an image of God which is then linked to a particular role for both the practitioner and the congregant, as well as the religious institution itself.

90

Transformation, eh?

Thursday, April 27, 2006

Sitting in the Zendo this morning, I lit a stick of incense and sat with it. Some say the incense turns into ash through combustion. Maybe so. But when sitting, there is just sitting. I read this morning that meditation could be "transformational." No doubt, just as burning turns incense "into" ash. But sitting is just sitting.

Incense is incense, burning is burning, ash is ash. Transformation is a mistake. It presumes too much and takes away from the real purpose of meditation which is precisely nothing. So, then, why practice the art of doing nothing? So that we can learn to be present with what is. Perhaps that is, in itself, transformative. Only practice will tell us.

91

Home Leaving

Friday, April 28, 2006

Home Leaving or Shukke in the Japanese, is about many things but should mostly be understood in its psychological and emotional sense. When we leave home we are literally leaving behind what we are comfortable with. All of our beliefs, our understandings, our connections near and dear, are left at our doorstep as we walk out into the desert. This preparatory act has been the same through millennia for those who are wishing to discover the deepest truths of existence. The Hebrews left Egypt, Moses left the Hebrews, Jesus went out in the desert for 40 days and nights, Buddha left his palace and wondered in the forests...when you think about it, every hero contemporary or historical, spiritual or materialist, leaves what they know in order to receive that which they do not know.

There is a relatively new Zen story about this. An American comes to Japan and seeks the teaching of a Zen Master. The Master pours tea. As the cup overflows, the would-be student shouts at the Master telling him that the cup is overflowing. The Master replies that the student must be empty to receive the teaching.

So, home leaving is about this.

Zazen is home leaving in the present moment. Zazen asks us to sit down quietly and be in the moment, not in yesterday's moment, not in the appearance of being in the moment, not in tomorrow's moment, but this very moment as it is, purely and directly. We cannot do this if we are carrying around our assumptions, our beliefs, and our values for security, or as a blanket or light against the darkness and cold.

To be in the presence of the infinite one must drop away the known and take a cavernous step into the unknown.

92

Remembrance

Saturday, April 29, 2006

Some say we should never forget the bad things that happen. They inform us of what humanity is actually capable of, giving us a true sense of our power and a large look at our morality. Some say the past should be a testimony, victims of atrocity should be given a voice. That voice should echo through time.

I am not so sure.

While remembrance serves the above functions, I truly wonder to what end? I know that it has not been particularly useful or helpful for me to retain traumatic memories of combat. Images of killing and death that seem eternally there in technicolor, are easily tripped and like a trip-flare the explode in graphic sensory stereo. Like I really need this in a crowd at Disney World.

We bow our heads and pray. We recite blessings, or mantras, and become synchronous with all history. We sit on meditation cushions or pews in a church or Temple and commune with the Infinite, remembering what is possible, actually what is, just now in this moment. And do what?

Remembrance Days are sort of like Departments of War. Self-fulfilling agencies of tears. I would rather we spend our money and brains on waging peace, finding non-violent alternatives to killing so no other generations need Remembrance Days.

We spend so much effort on such yesterday, so little on today. It's as if our lives are only meaningful when we wrap them in the past. Yet that is like being stuck in the mud. Some of us these days seem to enjoy their old mud, but not me. I want new mud, or more precisely, no mud at all.

93

The One and the Many

Sunday, April 30, 2006

As we each sit down on our cushions this morning, each of us drops away, the universe seems to enter, and all drops join the sea. The sea is constant, the drops are momentary. The sea is momentary, the drops are constant.

What this means is simple. Everything is both one and many, this one and many is nothing other than words in the theater of our mind however.

No one, not even the most solitary mountain hermit priest can be separate from anything. No one, not even in the most dense crowd is with others.

We are in each moment and are not in any other.

What does all this cryptic crap mean?

Sit Zazen and discover the truth for yourself.

94

Like Ash

Saturday, May 6, 2006

Multi-tasking is the great illness of the contemporary world. This disease is a result of attempting to do more with less and not being aware of doing any specific thing at all. It is a prescription for automated sleepwalking.

As workplaces demand more, people rise to the task, or so they believe. They pride themselves in being able to work on several operations at once, believing this will increase productivity and bear fruit in their lives. At home we multitask and fail to be present, not enjoying, just doing more for less.

The value of multitasking is a lie just as sure as the one told by Willie Loman in Death of a Salesman.

In fact, people who multitask do not task at all. They are non-sentient robots going through a set of motions and sometimes they wake up to discover their lives have all but disappeared, their children are grown and their spouses have found love and comfort elsewhere. Just as Willie Loman did.

Multitasking kills awareness. It anesthetizes the present moment. We do not truly live in this world of splintered attention. We splinter with our attention and become fragments of the human beings we are capable of being.

An old Zen teaching: There is wood, there is combustion, there is ash. It is a mistake to think of these as the same thing or part of a process. Wood is not turned into ash. Wood is wood. Ash is ash. Fire is fire. When we see process, we fail to see what is there before us, just as when we balance a checkbook while washing the dishes and attending to the children fails us from each: we are doing neither of these.

Choose to do less and accomplish more. Be present in your meeting, attend to your child, wash the dish: in each case establish a full presence in the situation. If this requires you to adjust your life, then perhaps less is more again.

In the end, how do you wish to be remembered? The person who was really there or the blur that could not be still?

95

What's to fear

Tuesday, May 9, 2006

How many of us can make a mistake without fear? Do we feel comfortable out of our comfort zone? Can we hear criticism and allow it to just lay there?

Most of us, perhaps all of us, cannot. We each have a strong need to be valued, appreciated, esteemed. Interaction with others (and sometimes even ourselves) makes this a challenge. Our culture is habituated toward critique.

Valuation is our livelihood. Discrimination our currency.

A statement suggesting what we say is off base or inaccurate invite rebuttal. If the rebuttal comes from fear, big problem. Fer creates defensive posturing. Fear closes us off from even looking at the merits of the suggestion: so strong is our need not to be wrong.

Why?

I am wrong often. I speak before I have the facts. I believe I know what someone is thinking or saying as they are speaking and formulate replies before they have finished their thought. I guess I think I'm a mind-reader or something. My father always charged me with being stupid and incompetent. I filter through his judgment. And just as surely as he is dead, so am I if I continue in this way.

Our practice is to be in this moment. Being in this moment requires courage as it demands we are open. Being open is a challenge when we are afraid. Yet our practice teaches us there is nothing to fear. There is no self to be abused, no feeling that will last forever (unless we keep it tightly stored and ready to use, and even then, it will die with us sometime).

It is a good practice to just be present without acting. In this practice allow yourself the luxury of not responding. Make a concerted effort to free your thoughts and let them float away. Those around you might be mystified, this behavior will be a small challenge for them, but I believe at some point this practice will bear fruit.

96

Stillness

Wednesday, May 10, 2006

Some of you have asked me to elaborate on the teaching of stillness. Let's try this: Create stillness right now. You are obviously at your computer just now.

Notice your breath. Where does it come from? Where does it go? Feel it as it enters and leaves your body.

Notice your eyes. Watch them as they move across the monitor.

Notice your mind. What it is up to? Questioning? Yawning?

Notice sound. Can you hear your computer? The sound of the refrigerator or air conditioner? Do you hear yourself swallow?

Notice what your mouth feels like inside. Is it moist? Dry? Where is your tongue? How do your teeth feel?

Notice your eyes blinking. Just witness them open and close.

Do nothing with anything you notice. Just let whatever is there be there and feel the stillness in your body. You do not have to immediately hit the delete key or the reply key or any other key.

When you are in the presence of others, you can do this as well. There is no law that says you must reply immediately. Take a few moments and witness yourself.

The most important aspect of this practice is attentive non-engagement.

When we practice this way, we should notice the need we seem to have to "do" something. Be careful of this need, it will usually lead to no good.

97

Unbearable

Thursday, May 11, 2006

The sun has once again risen and warmed the desert air. The coolness of the night evaporates quickly and we are left with hot, dry air. Where can we go to escape the heat?

What is the nature of unbearability? When we suffer and say "this is unbearable!" what do we mean? Our mind is intruding, demanding an alternative to the feelings experienced by our bodies or hearts. In some ways this is a good thing. Pain is an flag that causes us to look and act to be safe or well.

Yet all of these are mental formations, constructs that have no independent existence. They come and go like the breeze or the sun. We suffer in direct proportion to our desire not to suffer. The more we imagine non-suffering and compare that imagined state to that which we abide, we suffer.

When it is hot we wish to be cool. When we are cold, we wish to be warm. All of this wishing separates us from our present moment experience. It creates a gulf between us and reality.

Our practice is to not rant against the heat but simply be. We can move to the shade, without thinking about escaping the heat. We can enjoy the heat.

We can recognize that heat and cold are relative states to us, the subject. We can join the heat and in so doing allow it to lose its power.

And so it is with life.

98

The News and the Spirit

Sunday, May 13, 2006

The morning news is bothersome, as always. People killed. Explosions. Domestic spying. Lawsuits. Sometimes it is good practice to avoid the newspaper and internet news services. The type and level of information, speed of delivery, and tone is poisonous to the spirit.

Yet we don't really want to live as ostriches.

It is important to know your world and the happenings within it. It is important to know what your government is doing, how it is doing it, and the goals it claims in the process. Our government does not seem to be as forthcoming as it might be. We are fighting a war, it claims.

Remember the works of fiction that warned us in school? 1984, Brave New World, Player Piano (the first Kurt Vonnegut jr. book which was quite interesting in light of today's world)?

Here we are. Of course it's not the same. The threats are real. And so are the psychological processes of leading through fear. Like lemmings, we are willingly giving up our rights to privacy. We are giving up our money and many of our freedoms to wage wars of peace and end fear and intimidation by Third World sets of people wanting to bring back the Middle Ages.

I am one who believes terror wins when we decide to become fearful, hiding, and secretive. A brave society is a society that remains free and above board even when threatened. A compassionate society cares about our enemies, nurtures the poor and the weak regardless of race, creed, or national origin. A smart society lives beyond superstition and the fear of fundamentalists and their devil.

When your heart is closed, you die regardless of whether you are safe. When your heart is open, you live even if you are in danger.

99

Charity

Sunday, May 14, 2006

The first of the Six Paramitas is Dana, or Generosity. I enjoy this paramita very much as it reminds me that to be generous means to be so without self. Any reminder to drop away self is a good thing. We spend so much of our day wrapped up in ourselves that to get out of the wrapper is actually quite liberating.

In the Diamond Sutra, the Buddha taught that a man should "bestow alms, uninfluenced by any pre-conceived thoughts as to self and other selves..." and if in "practicing charity, conceives within his mind...conceptions discriminating himself from other selves, he will be like a man walking in darkness and seeing nothing." (Goddard translation, p.90-91).

This has some very specific meaning and teaching. Similar to the Christian notion that if a man asks for a coat, you should also give him your cloak. Thought to self, and judgment as to the worthiness of others has no place in these teachings. The moment self enters, judgment and discernment enter, we are in the darkness and delusion of dualism. The heart of the Buddha's teaching is compassion for others as a starting point and an end in itself. In this sense, then, we enter charity and become charity, within this charity there is no me, no you, no beggar or almsgiver. Being generosity is being Buddha. Another definition of Mutual Aid.

100

Fences

Tuesday, May 16, 2006

Ever since I was a little kid I wondered how borders existed. I often looked at maps of the world, scouring the continents, looking at the lines separating one country from another and wondering what they looked like on the ground. As a kid I thought maybe there were actual lines and that it must be somebody's job to go around painting them, like they do on roads. As an adult I still wonder about these lines dividing us as a species. I wonder about how these divisions divide us rather than bring us together. I wonder about the fear that is created through groupings, the discrimination that develops, and often think about the world as a place without boundary as a place without limits.

When we drop our boundaries, in one sense, we create possibilities for expansion. Companies know this. International corporations see boundaries as impediments and actively work within them to make them non-existent. Would it not be wise to eventually find a way to live on this planet as if we are all part of the same family of man?

Creating fences, putting armed soldiers along our borders, seems unwise to me. It creates a police state of sorts and further divides us. True security, it seems to me, comes with friendship and intermarriage, where all people see themselves as family.

Threats to the family will always exist, well at least as long as there are both vast differences between haves and have-nots and as long as groups of people suffer and die while others live and thrive. Increasing the height of the fence will not stop that.

101

Defining the Spiritual Situation

Wednesday, May 17, 2006

So, we have a continuum of understanding of God from "No God" on one side to "God" on the other with a thousand shades of gray in between. Each shade presents its own unique hue, its own understanding of the role of the "believer" and the "clergy." Each contains its own "domain assumptions."

Manuel argues that we Buddhists are above and beyond a notion of God. This might be one side of the continuum. Understanding the issue, of course, from the subject's point of view. Do I want to even acknowledge the possibility of an object, subject asks? The Buddha himself seemed to want to avoid these discussions because he felt they were not useful to the goal of the Buddha Way. They are of the sort that philosophers often get to: how many angels can dance on the head of a pin?

Yet my commentary is not so metaphysical. It is quite practical.

Our understanding of the universe guides us. Our willingness to drop away self and be enfolded by all is an important ingredient to our daily practice. The idea of God is clearly a human invention, and in primitive cultures this idea was anthropomorphized so that we could either better understand our conception of God or control him through supplication.

Some have argued that God is none other than a reflection of ourselves and so has evolved as have we through the centuries. No doubt this is true. And if true, where are we today?

To dismiss God dismisses entire cultures and their very powerful beliefs. Dismissing this means not understanding those cultures and such a lack of understanding can be deadly, especially in the contemporary climate. Jihad is, after all, a "holy war."

None of my discussion was intended to argue for or against a personal belief or point of view, only that we use a frame of reference within which we might understand how various peoples use God or a notion of God in their lives. Even atheists have a God they rail against, otherwise they would be mute. Often their understanding of such a God is of the Judeo-Christian variety, often punitive and primitive in conception. Such a notion becomes a straw man in an argument and suggests a simplistic examination of the whole thing.

God, however, is a universal phenomenon, not constrained by the human mind, not created in the human mind. God as the universe, the intricate processes, the outside and the inside, the very fabric of existence, is hardly an anthropomorphism. We in Zen might understand God as Shunyata itself. Or not.

102

Rich Beyond Measure

Monday, May 22, 2006

Over the last few days I have been practicing mindfulness in motion. Practices this as a participant-witness through my day, moving, sitting, eating, talking, listening with full attention. This full attention is special, however, as it is attention without effort. Just witnessing the breath, the sound, the smell, the sight, the mental imaginings, all the while knowing that they are unreal is the truest sense.

I listen now to the baby giggle, then cry, and the delicate chopping and slicing sounds of my son's knife as it expertly cuts through myriad fresh vegetables and herbs as he prepares our evening meal. The conditioned air flows across my face and through the hair of my newly growing beard on my face.

In each moment a lifetime of experiences.

We are so rich, each of us. The whole world of experience is ours for the willingness to touch it. It is such a shame that we withdraw so often, blunt our senses, and cloud our minds with the clippity-clap of notions.

Live awake.

103

Karma

Wednesday, May 24, 2006

If you, me, and the universe are one then what is the real teaching of karma?

To address this question you must really enter it. You, me, and the universe are products of dualistic thought, convenient and necessary for survival, but weights on the rope of liberation. Karma is nothing other than an understanding of the deep and continuous connections of everything. Often thought of as cause and effect, we understand karma when we mentally step away and see that streams flow in all directions at once.

This is because that is. Very precise. Very exacting. Nothing is individual or separate or unnecessary. When you are this teaching, karma is just another useless notion, like heaven and hell, nirvana and samsara, you and me, or the many other rafts along the shore.

104

Just Do

Thursday, May 25, 2006

So, you are busy. Too busy to take good care of yourselves. And then you die. Whatever you were busy with no longer matters a whole lot.

The most important thing?

In the meantime, life happens. Between the tasks, at the stoplight, during a break, sipping a cup of water, just before you speak, these are the moments we are most awake these days. The rest of the time life seems not to be our own. We place ourselves on autopilot and just get through.

This is no way to live.

Stop it. Live in every moment, as you do your task, do it completely; as you drive, drive mindfully; as you speak, speak with care. This is not difficult, but it does take practice. Sometimes you will be there, sometimes not. It's OK, just do.

105

Show and Tell

Friday, May 26, 2006

There is a phrase a Korean Zen Master used frequently: Open mouth already a mistake!

This is so true. Language and the workings of our minds to produce language and the thought behind it, is essentially dualistic. There is no getting around it. This is why many koans have no literal, verbal answer and why so often the Master asks the student to "show" him rather than "tell" him.

Even in literature this is true, oddly enough. We are asked to show something in our stories and poems, rather than tell something. Pictures, painted or spoken, are better than a thousand words spewed out.

Moreover, the moment we open our mouths to speak we are out of the moment and into our thoughts about the moment. Yet we struggle so with this, I know I do.

I want to tell you!

Yet in doing so, I make a big mistake.

You must teach yourself!

You must experience yourself!

There is no telling that is worth anything. From whence does this desire to tell come?

106

Stay Small

Saturday, May 27, 2006

Simple tasks make all the difference. Sip coffee. Sit quietly. Water a plant. Avoid stepping on an ant. When we stay small we stay awake.

Keep this in mind.

107

Nothing Holy

Sunday, May 28, 2006

Throughout most of the day yesterday I burnt incense. I sat Zazen off and on throughout the day and late last night.

My mother is in the hospital and was told she does not have long to live.

What does one do with such news. Her lungs and heart are very weak and not functioning very well. She has decided against heroic measures, claiming she is ready to die. We talked a couple of times at length about everything. She has made her peace.

We are neither born nor do we die. We neither come nor do we go. In truth, there is no "we" in such matters. These are all just constructs of a mind hardwired to see linear events discreetly. Yet, as Master Bodhidharma once answered, "Vast emptiness. Nothing holy."

We should add, nothing profane.

Profane and sacred are one, just as life and death are one. In this sense, the ancient Hebrews had it dead-on:

Adonai Eloheinu, Adonai Echad! (The Lord our God, the Lord is One).

What we do with such news is we live!

108

A Stolen Buddha is a Lesson

Tuesday, May 30, 2006

There was a story in the local newspaper this morning about a statue of the Buddha being recovered after it was stolen. The last paragraph reads "...Buddhists also believe in karma, which says a person's actions in this life determine the quality of their existence in the next."

Yes and no.

This is an example of how language and culturally infused meanings become problematic. Buddhists also "believe" that there is no soul, no substance, that transmigrates from one life to another. Thus, a contradiction.

Buddhists also "believe" there is no birth and no death. Therefore no this life, no next life. Another contradiction.

What are we to do? A Zen Teacher would shout:

Practice Zazen. See your true nature for yourself. Look deeply into the heart of the matter!

We Americans hate this sort of thing! We want to *know* and we want to know NOW!

Otherwise, the Teacher is not teaching and the whole thing is just tooooo mysterious! (Or better still, *esoteric*)

To borrow a short, but succinct word from another tradition, "Oy!"

Here's the thing. Lives are constant, there are no breaks between them. I am "born" from cells developed in my mother's uterus, my cells merge with another's cells to form another being that individuates and is "born" and so on. There is no point where I am or was not. We get stuck when we use "I" as a point of reference rather than the universe at large. When seen from the larger, universal perspective, life is organically rising and falling and rising again: always at all times. In this process of rising and falling, the parts have roles to play.

As parts of this universal process, we can make our universe a better place or a worse place for all of the other parts. Since we are all constant parts of this one vast universal process, parts past and parts present, we are rendering karma.

We are way too egocentric to see this without much practice. Those living in the Far East on the other hand have grown up with a more universal and collective understanding of their existence with much less emphasis on the individual "part."

Isn't life interesting?

109

Bearing Witness

Thursday, June 1, 2006

Bearing witness is a challenging practice. Many do not wish to see witnesses, few wish to be reminded of things past. Witnesses become our consciences and how many of us truly appreciate that voice in our ear? We assign motives to the witnesses, we can even grow to despise them. We confuse the witness with the event itself and akin to the messenger, want to kill the witness.

To bear witness under these conditions becomes a strength building practice and an important practice in itself.

Yesterday at the weekly Peace Vigil, I sat quietly on my cushion on the sidewalk. The sun was very hot and my robes offered protection from the burning rays, but also allowed the air under them to heat. Zen priest sauna.

I listened as the birds chatter in the trees of the courthouse courtyard. I listened to someone tell the story that earlier in the war, counter-protesters were across the street. One person set up a sign a few blocks away that read, "Terrorists Ahead, Fire at Will!"

The witness, in the end, must simply be present. Rather like being with a very sick person or someone who is dying. We are just present and that presence is, in itself, healing.

In this presence, however, our inclination is to want to 'do something' as if our mere presence as a witness is not enough. Resist this temptation. Listen to your mind as you are sitting as witness. Watch the mental flow, the feelings arise and fall, give them nothing.

When we witness this way we are most effective. We are just peace. We are just compassion. Nothing else.

110

What do you see?

Friday, June 2, 2006

Today I will drive up to the Refuge. I look forward to this drive, as well as to getting there. The drive across the desert from the city is really beautiful. The desert can be very subtle. The colors are so muted and because the sky is so large and unimpeded, a very different scale of relative size is present. People coming here for the first time often just see vast expanses of brown. I know I did. But then, as time goes by and our senses acclimate to the place, we begin to really "see" the desert for the first time.

Such is life. We often see in gross terms and only later see the details and nuances that enrich our lives. It is our practice to make the distance between the gross and the subtle non-existent.

111

Where's Buddha?

Sunday, June 4, 2006

Yesterday I was re-reading a tiny little book by Senzaki. He was a Japanese monk who came to America before there was much in the way of Zen here. He was a wanderer, not affiliated with a home temple, and despised what he called "Cathedral Zen." Cathedral Zen is the Zen of large Temples, rich patrons, and lavish pomp and circumstance. There is a tendency to move in this direction among American Zen Centers.

Americans like their Churches, Synagogues and Mosques to be large and ostentatious. We have the idea that if it is large and rich it must be doing something right and everyone wants to hang on to a winner. Yet even when full these places are empty. Something essential is missing.

True Zen begins as a temple of one and works its way out. True Zen is free. It is the color of the grass, the feel of the sand, the taste of a cold cucumber on a hot summer day. It has nothing to do with robes and bells, priests and laymen. We put on a robe, shave our head, sit Zazen because we are buddhas, not to become like buddhas.

Today be the buddha you are in everything you do. How is that possible? Be yourself.

112

Facing a day, Facing Yourself

Monday, June 5, 2006

Monday morning. Its a beautiful day. Many of us approach Monday as if we were climbing a mountain with sacks of rocks on our backs. Working at jobs that seem to work against us, our sense of accomplishment and personal worth challenged, we feel disheartened and even disconnected.

Others go to work with a sense of hope and joy, embracing their work, making it a part of them and their experience in the world. They have a sense of personal power and control, a sort of personal authority that enables real authenticity to develop.

What are the differences between these people?

Is it the work itself? Their peers? Their employers or supervisors? Is it something in the water?

So many variables. Yet one major variable comes to mind: Right Understanding. Right Understanding is a sort of synchronicity, an orientation of compass, map, and traveler. Once oriented, it is possible to make sense of where we are, what direction to go, what degree of effort it will take, how much of what needs to be said, and so forth. People living without Right Understanding are like travelers at war with their compasses and maps.

As in each of the Eightfold Noble Paths, "Right" refers to "true, perfect, same." Understood as we are using the word here, then, we orient ourselves with our compass and our map, making them "true." True here means many things, but mostly it means "the same." That is to say, when we become one with our activity, like an arrow flying true to its mark, where arrow and mark are, in truth one, then we are living within Right Understanding.

Who are you? What is your compass? What is your map? How are you not one?

113

As You Are

Wednesday, June 7, 2006

The sun is just now peeking out over the building next door to my Zendo window. I feel its heat on my face. There is something so reassuring about the sun rising in the morning. I have written about this before. For me it signals that I can relax. I've made it through the night.

For many of us, going to sleep does not mean we will for certain wake up again. Coming to sleep with this attitude is only possible when we are at peace with this moment. We must be willing to say and believe completely, this is enough. I have such an understanding, but it was not always so. Striving and desiring, craving for another day to make my mark, to do something wonderful, or to avoid a mistake, fix a problem, these were feelings that got in the way of rest.

With life, however, our true sphere of influence is revealed. It begins and ends in our own skin. Our true task is to master that sphere. With this realization, the wonder of a simple breath takes on incredible significance. The beauty of sitting at a desk or walking down a corridor or listening to a talk or building something or unpacking something becomes the beginning and the end: it is, in itself, fully and completely sufficient.

I am learning to feel what is there. The plastic keys of this computer, its casing as I rest my fingers and palms between words and thoughts, are each complete moments in themselves worthy of both recognition and respect. To do this well means recognizing the slippery slope of mental travel and letting the slope be by itself.

114

Pacify my Mind!

Friday, June 9, 2006

As a student, the second patriarch asks Bodhidharma to pacify his mind. An odd sort of question to ask of a teacher, don't you think? Well, maybe not. Today Zen Teachers and Therapists are both asked the same question, framed differently: how can I be happy? Or I need something, I mean I really need something and it's out of my reach. Help me reach it!

Old Bodhidharma asked this student to search for his mind and bring it to him, he would then pacify it.

So, off the student goes, searching for this mind to be pacified.

The search is a turbulent one. Where is this mind that is sooo demanding? Today, students and clients do the same. Good teachers and good therapists ask their supplicants to search out that which is driving them crazy. And of course, they come back with the same line our second patriarch did, "I cannot find it."

There, says Bodhidharma, I have pacified it.

To understand this story, we must see the source of distress. Distress is not "out there" somewhere to be found. Distress is a personal thing originating in the very mechanics of our bodies. We seek what we imagine and like the ends of rainbows, imaginings are ever illusive. The moment we see the fundamental truth of this is the moment we are free of it.

A good teacher, like a good therapist, gives the student what the student needs, but not necessarily as the student first perceives it.

115

Passion

Saturday, June 10, 2006

Is there a fire in your life? A passion that draws you, demands that you wake and get out of bed? Is it raging? Is it smoldering? How do you recognize it? How do you feel about it? What do you do with it?

Is this fire a good thing or a bad thing?

These are life questions, important to both our happiness and our quality of life. As Viktor Frankl pointed out years ago, we cannot exist as human beings without meaning in our lives. Yet is meaning and our search for it, the same as this fire?

Most of us live with something we feel passionate about, if only our spouse or children (not to suggest these are small things). Some of us are fortunate to work in fields we feel passionate about. In such cases work is not work, but life itself. Others feel passionate about the world and its condition. We live to repair it, to bring it to life, to heal it, to make the world a better place.

In whatever context this passion arises, it must be balanced. Tempering our passions is like tempering steel. We fold the steel over and over, pounding it, folding it, pounding it, folding it, until the moment it becomes a fine blade. With each folding the steel must rest. There is a time for heat, a time for pounding, a time for folding, and a time for rest. So too with what we love.

It would be a good practice for each of us to address the questions at the top of this post then ask ourselves how we balance and integrate these into our lives.

116

Wrestling with Whatever

Monday, June 12, 2006

What are we here for? Why do we exist? Is there indeed a purpose to our existence?

Thinking like this leads us to the sky.

Such questions.

Who knows. Who cares!

We are here. That's what matters. Or does it?

Thinking like this leads us to the earth.

What matters even more?

What happens when earth and sky come together.

Philosophy and religion have always grappled with such things, as has mythology. Sky beings, lofty, wise, untouched and untouchable on one hand; earth beings, crude, dirty, and wet on the other hand.

For philosophy, these were points of departure. The original mind conceiving and then laying out conception: maybe Hegelian, maybe Epicurean. Yet, in literature and mythology, including the stories of the bible, Zen, we see these two wrestling.

The Epic of Gilgamesh, that five-thousand-year-old Babylonian drama, casts Gilgamesh the light prince engaging Enkidu the earth demon. Jacob wrestles with God. Beowulf wrestles with Grendel, Buddha wrestles with Mara. In all of these, it is the wrestling that matters.

Nothing is clear cut. Nothing is one way or the other. The universe is a sloppy, wet, muddy affair. Yet there are rocks to climb on so that we may dry off and rest for a bit. One such rock might be your church or mosque, yet another, your cushion. In any event the real wrestling resides within.

Cherish it.

117

That Old Tree

Tuesday, June 13, 2006

O Shariputra, remember, Dharma is fundamentally emptiness, no birth, no death. Nothing is pure, nothing is defiled. Nothing can increase, nothing can decrease. Hence: in emptiness, no form, no feeling no thought, no impulse, no consciousness; no eye, no ear, no nose, no tongue, no body, no mind; no seeing, no hearing, no smelling, no tasting, no touching, no thinking, no realm of sight, no realm of thought, no ignorance and no end of ignorance, no old age and death and no end to old age and death. No suffering, no craving, no extinction, no path, no wisdom, no attainment.

This scriptural teaching from the Great Heart of Wisdom Sutra, suggests all of the things we believe are real are just concepts created in our minds. They have no meaning apart from that meaning we apply. We must be careful, therefore in our application of, and wedding to, this meaning. We must see it for what it is, a convenience, a shorthand, a tool, but most of all, an invention.

When we can move freely from form to no form, realizing birth and death are artificial constructs, living with both purity and impurity as places upon a single plane of existence, then we are truly free.

Clinging to any one of these concepts becomes a knife that cleaves the universe in two.

If a tree falls in the forest, does it make a sound?

Sound is audible, sound is a name for something audible. For audible to be, there must be ears to hear. For name to be, there must be a mind to both name and recognize name. No sense organs, no sense.

So, does a tree falling in the forest make a sound?

118

Six of One

Wednesday, June 14, 2006

Wisdom requires meditative living, meditative living requires diligence, diligence requires patience, patience requires a moral sensibility, a moral sensibility requires generosity.

The paramitas are one.

Let's suppose that you were to spend one day a week on each paramita, with one day off for good behavior. That's not so difficult. Get up in the morning, read something relating to the paramita of the day, sit Zazen with that paramita in mind. Drive to work with that paramita, enacting it as you can, seeing where it fits or doesn't fit, how it can be applied or not, and so on.

If you spent that entire day examining it as it applies to your actual life, then at the end of a year you will have spent 52 days developing each of these excellences in your life. Fifty-two days of generosity of morality, of patience, of diligence, of meditation, and of wisdom.

What a year, what a person.

119

Making the Coffee

Saturday, June 17, 2006

The desert air is cool this morning, a mere 70 degrees. I am sitting here under the ceiling fan enjoying the air flowing over my shoulders. The orchid on my desk is amazing, beautiful yellow backgrounds splashed with magenta. Both dogs are sleeping and Pete-kitty is rolled up in a small ball near My Little Honey's pillow.

The most wonderous things are present if we stop to appreciate them. This stopping requires of us a willingness to just be there. We are not to disturb. We are not to enter. We are present.

When we are present, we experience being in the cool, in the air, in the presence of the universe. It's the difference of being in the flow as opposed to being against the flow.

Yet here's the thing. When your little honey gets up and asks where's the coffee is, you don't get defensive, you don't get wrinkled, instead, you walk into the kitchen and make the coffee.

Seamless.

120

An Edge

Sunday, June 18, 2006

As we live out our lives, many of us have the propensity to live on the darker edges of things. As residents of the edge we see the contrasts between light and dark. We taste delight and revulsion. We are right there on that edge!

Some are energized in a morose sort of way while there. Others become lethargic and nihilistic: nothing matters.

This edge can be a real blessing or a source of true torture.

It is a place without a future. It flails the past. It makes the present a dark stew.

Those who see clearly the truth of life and death are tempted to accept this edge and make it home. Wrapping themselves in their robes of futility and acceptance they rot like the corpses they are.

The others with clouded minds dance like moths on the tip of the flame. Exquisite.

Followers of the Great Way, though, step off the edge. They have faith in the universe and know their way is not to sit on the edge, but to walk in the world doing what needs to be done. Hungry person? Feed him. Cold person? Give him a blanket. Glass breaks on the floor? Sweep it up. Dog wants out? Take him out.

When your moral conscience is in your body, there is no question.

121

Hate

Monday, June 19, 2006

The Buddha said: Hatreds do not ever cease in this world by hating, but by not hating; this is an eternal truth.

And how easy is that!

This is a core practice. We know that thoughts of ill will arise. We see this every day, indeed, we experience this every day. Zazen teaches us that these thoughts and their concomitant feelings come but also go. Zazen teaches us that by residing in stillness, even while in motion, we do not enact ill will.

The Buddha is stating a behavioral truth here. We can change our heart by changing our behavior. If we choose not to enact hate, we will reduce and eventually eliminate hate from our minds and hearts. Just so, if we decide not to swear, swearing will become less a habit of mind and heart.

The eternal truth here is that mind, heart, and body are one.

Replace hate with love and there's a possibility that its good medicine will heal the world, one being at a time.

122

A Rainbow

Wednesday, June 21, 2006

Enlightenment. Powerful word. Lots of people searching for it, most with only a vague feeling as to what it is. Which creates a question in my mind. If we do not have a clear idea as to what this is, why are we searching for it?

My sense is that enlightenment means many things to many people. So they search in myriad directions and along many paths. Some see enlightenment as a sort of higher plane of existence. We might understand it as holding hands with God or deeply abiding with the universe. Some see it as an escape from suffering. Others see it as bliss. And still others a sense of seeing clearly. Many things.

The thing is, the search is the problem. To search means that we are looking. This activity is steeped in dualism.

So, what do we do?

Nothing. We aspire to enlightenment, sit still with that aspiration, and let ourselves be present. There is really nothing to seek that we don't already possess. Perhaps it is this acceptance, on its deepest level, that is truly 'enlightenment.'

123

A Desert Wind, A Concrete Wall

Friday, June 23, 2006

Yesterday we had a wind come across the desert down off the mountains. Those who live 'back east' or in other parts of the world may not understand what a "wind" means. Let me say that its rather like being present in a wind tunnel. Desert winds are often sustained and go through the day and night.

To be present in such wind means there is no real escaping it. The sound is just there, along with the air pressure and its other manifestations. I once ran a full marathon into such a wind.

Like the heat, or noise, or hustle of all the rest of our environmental challenges to our serenity, we must learn to be in the challenge itself. Once we exist within the challenge, no challenge can exist, as challenge.

This is so difficult, yet so simple. Challenge, difficulty, trouble or bother: all are mental constructs. All are statements suggesting a value we bring to the situation. We do not like such and such! Go away! How can I be peaceful when the whole world is at war?!!!

Two things. Recognize that our attitude or orientation means everything. When we accept the wind as a fact of our life, appreciate it for what it is, join the noise so to speak, no problem. Second, we cannot change the world all at once or even a little at a time. All we can do is change within ourselves and allow that change to bloom in the world itself.

So, how does one step into a concrete wall?

124

Inside-Out Zen

Sunday, June 25, 2006

There can be a serious precision to our practice that gets in the way of awakening, as well as compassionate living. Some people become so caught in the net of this and that, the 2 centimeters of difference, that they fail to see the Buddha's face.

One of the truths of monastic practice is that life in a group can be a real challenge to serenity, but then we all know that don't we? It is easy to be a Buddha alone and undisturbed by the ticking of the clock or the needs of a baby. Some practitioners, especially those who revere monastic practice, view the exactitude of ritual as very important. Order on the outside rules.

Another finger pointing.

What is important is the inside out. I like inside-out Zen. Our precision is from the inside. That is to say, our internal to external correspondence to the Buddha and his attributes are the thing most important. But then, how do we get there?

On the one hand we can say that ritualized practice, the forms, so to speak, offer us a vessel within which we train ourselves. This is outside-in Zen.

On the other hand, our zazen of mind and body, establishing from the inside the strength and discipline to sit upright, is inside-out Zen.

Of course, at some point along the way, we attain there is little difference. Inside and outside are the same.

Do not be so critical with yourself.

125

Splash!

Monday, June 26, 2006

In Zen we see heart, mind, and body as one, indeed, all of the universe is this body. Nice thought, a great truth, but thoughts about truth are not the experience of truth. To experience this truth, we must stop behaving as if we are separate.

How does one behave as if one is not separate?

This is the point of so many Zen stories and koans. Each story, each koan, points us at something. It asks us to understand by getting into the story and in order to get into the story, we must become the story.

Yet here we are again, how does one become the story? Or the koan?

Just how does one "drop away"?

I once had an art teacher who was into empathy. She had use drawing old weird leaves. We were told to "feel the leaf," "become the leaf," and so on. I thought she was nuts. So, I sat there, good student that I was, and drew the leaf. We were taught to draw by keeping our eye on the object and not on the paper and ink. Staying on the object, following its line this way and that, to the point that there was only the line: no eye, no hand, no pen, no...ahhh.

It is counter intuitive. To let the self drop away means to practice joining non-self. To think non-thinking means to practice non-thinking. Following the lines until we attain there are no lines and no one to follow them.

It's like jumping into a pool.

126

Does the Fan Disturb the Air?

Tuesday, June 27, 2006

The windows are open and the ceiling fans are slowly turning. The morning air here is cool. The sound of the fan against the still morning air is soft. I wonder about the stillness of zazen.

Someone asked last night, "Can we go deeper?"

Such an interesting question. Zazen as a practice of plumbing the depths, or of mining the earth for its riches. I suppose, but what is deeper? What is behind the question?

We sit zazen for a variety of reasons, all of us. We sit with a variety of intentions, as many as there are sitting buddhas, I am sure. Yet, on this meditation cushion and in this stillness, we seem to settle, some may say 'sink', deeper and deeper into the stillness. So, it often seems as though we are, indeed, 'going deeper.'

I wonder though if it could not be understood slightly differently, that instead of going deeper we are just shedding the many layers we use to clothe our 'self' and in the shedding, come ever closer to seeing ourselves as the universe itself.

Can we go deeper? We are vast emptiness itself; we just need to stop isolating ourselves with wrappings of identity.

127

One Born Every Minute

Wednesday, June 28, 2006

We have all heard the phrase, "there's one born every minute!" This "one" typically refers to a sucker, a hapless, gullible person, who is easily taken advantage of. None of us want to be seen by others as such a one. We are all too smart or too sophisticated, too sharp, or too quick and nimble to be "taken" by the con artists of the world.

When we divide our fellow man like this, into the gullible and the nimble & quick, where is charity? Where is compassion? Where is loving-kindness?

There is no room for these qualities, as they become marks of the hapless ones.

Interesting isn't it, how our intelligent, high tech, and efficient society has recast discrimination? A discriminating mind now is highly valued, protected, and to be therefore cultivated.

So, today, the "one" more appropriately should be thought of as a "critic."

Yes, there is one born every minute.

128

Weebles

Thursday, June 29, 2006

If we could see around corners, we would never get hit. But we cannot see around corners, so we must be cautious. I wonder.

When we are one with the universe, where is a corner?

Caution is like a weeble, tilting to and fro, but never actually getting anywhere.

A True Master understands there is no birth and death, just this. A True Master is the Buddha inside and out. The Infinite and Finite are one and without a blink of an eye. A True Master is both giver and receiver at once and at the same moment. A True Master is both love and hate, peace and war, all residing in serene reflection.

We call this authority, and being one with it, we call manifest Buddha.

129

Repairing the World

Friday, June 30, 2006

Last evening at a meeting someone said they did not want politics in their house of worship. They argued that they come to Temple for refuge and that there were plenty of groups and activities "out there" who would gladly accept our help, why bring these issues into the Temple? She was referring to the Jewish Temple.

I have heard this argument in Zen Centers as well. And I am sure they are voiced in Christian churches, and Mosques, and wherever people gather together to connect to the Universe. Yet, in every major religion, there will come a time in its practice where it must move from the inside out.

Christianity has a strong missionary thrust, sometimes to my dismay, Judaism has a very long history of holding that they have a partnership with God to "repair the world," that is, to act as co-creators, finishing the work of creation. Buddhism has a very strong social and ethical commitment and recognizes that we ourselves create evil, as well as good, and therefore must act to support the choice for good.

Most of the people who want to keep politics out of the sanctuary are really saying that they need a sanctuary, free from strife and division. They seek a place without acrimony and negative, derisive, emotion. And for this, I can agree. But if we leave it there, we are failing these individuals. Our practice community, our Sangha, is a microcosm of the world itself. We practice within it, bringing to it all of what we are, our hopes, fears and dreams, as well as our prejudices and delusions. Chief among these is the notion that there is somehow an inside and an outside, an us and a them.

One of the tests of authentic practice is how consistently syntonic it is. We say we vow to stop doing evil, to do good, and to bring about good in the world (and every faith tradition has vows or prayers similar to these concise vows), but the test is how much they are expressions of ourselves.

As a religious or philosophical person, we must take our belief, faith, our practices, if they are authentic, out into the world. We must stand for the good against evil. Good and evil are not amorphous concepts. They are practical and political realities.

It takes a certain faith to accomplish this. Sometimes we must pretend, so to speak, talking the talk until our walk is more firm and centered. This takes time and commitment to the faith and values of our tradition. It also takes great strength and courage, but most of all it takes a great and growing love for the world.

130

When Worlds Collide

Saturday, July 1, 2006

A somewhat tumultuous conversation after services last night led me to think a lot about consistency of values and actions. If one holds themselves out to be a person of faith and that faith calls for or points to certain values, then we should attempt to behave according to those values. So goes the story line. On the other hand, we each must come to our own values through our own spiritual work. It appears that spiritual work or reflection is no guarantee that common values will emerge. And then what? We cannot discount the values we oppose. We cannot dictate values. Yet, at the same time a group's cohesiveness often depends on shared values.

So, what are we to do?

One thought I had is that people might begin speaking of only what their values are, rather than what others should not value. This will at least give us a set of values cast as positives. From this list of values, we could select those we believe are either worthy of our attention or less worthy of our attention and then work on objectives and goals.

Of course, the problem with such a plan is that it ignores the crux of the issue: ethical dilemmas. An ethical dilemma occurs when two values of equal merit conflict with one another. Such an example might include a woman's right to choose what happens to her own body versus the value of life. Or the value of freedom on the one hand and the value of peace on the other.

Traditionally value conflicts or ethical dilemmas are dealt with by two types of resolution, a deontological perspective and a consequentialist perspective. A deontological approach is rules based, such as those within Judaism: a set of commandments decides. A consequentialist approach looks at what happens if each of the two paths to a conflict are taken, attempts to weigh the consequences for all concerned, and selects the path that leads to the greater good over bad for most of the people involved.

Yikes. Another problem! What happens to those people who hold a value, such as non-violence and others are able to establish the moral supremacy of their value, armed intervention?

We might say that some values are universal, peace, for example. But is peace always a universal value? This is the heart of true spiritual practice, in my opinion.

It is to those who engage in this true spiritual practice that I bow.

131

The Truth is Out There?

Monday, July 3, 2006

Have you ever noticed how things change? Of course you have, it happens that we notice this so often, we've developed phrases for it: things change, whatever, so it goes, and so on. Yet, what we don't so often notice is just how much energy we put into keeping absolutes permanent. We want some things not to change, truth, for example. We want something we perceive to be true to stay that way. Otherwise, our world would be a relativistic nightmare, we fear. Yes, we need our anchors.

The trouble is we look for anchors in all the wrong places. We look for them, first of all, as if they exist somewhere out there. We reify them, make them concrete and hard, like a statue or a note from God on a tablet made of stone. At this point we decide these are, indeed, the truth and the truth must be defended. And so it goes.

Yet, when we bother to examine truth closely what do we see? We see that truth always depends on the perceiver. Truth is, by definition, a mental construction. It does not exist independent of us. Therefore, it is something we have invented to perceive, an overlay of sorts, like a gel used in theater to color a subject.

So where to look for truth and what is its true nature?

Here's a twister: the absolute truth is always relative to a context. We can say killing is wrong and that is an absolute truth and that would be true, but at the same time we must understand that the context of this absolute is the context of the value we place on life. So if life is being threatened and there is no other way to prevent it from being killed, we must kill the threat.

Second. Context is always subjective and relative. Context depends on a perceiver and perceivers exist in context with one another: they are, therefore relative. Some may argue that absolutes exist, by nature apart from a perceiver. To those I would ask, show me an absolute that could be understood without a context.

We begin with being still and we end in that stillness. Knowing that the stillness is not something out there, but something we are, as being itself. Stillness is not "running" when we are running. Stillness is not "working" when we are working. Nor is stillness "sitting" when we are sitting. Truth, like stillness, is both universal and relative. Hold onto it and it becomes false.

132

Independence Day

Tuesday, July 4, 2006

Hoopla today in the USA. Independence Day should give us pause to be thankful of the things independence from oppression offers us. Yet this independence is conditional, it always is. We are never independent, as if we are standalone entities, pulling ourselves up by our bootstraps. This most profound and basic statement of American value contains a fatal flaw. Someone must make the boots, the pants, and the shirts we wear. Someone must drill for the oil we burn, grow and harvest the food we eat, make the chemicals and do the magic that creates the plastic that forms so much the framework of our lives.

We celebrate our independence from oppression here today yet live deeply oppressed. What's the name of the boot on our neck? Desire. True independence is our awakening to our true interdependence.

133

Far from Buddha

Thursday, July 6, 2006

When we study the precepts, we are entering the study of moral life. We sometimes think of morality as a tricky thing. But I say, the only tricky part is getting caught between the things we want or don't want and wanting or not wanting them both at the same time. Of course, Philosophy 101 classes and Ethics classes are full of those arguing about what is good and what is evil. Or which I should do, honor the principle or support the greater good. We look to our group, family, or culture for answers. Is this the "Christian" thing to do? The Buddhist thing? The Jewish thing? We sometimes have guiding questions, "what would Jesus do?" Or, "what would Buddha do?" We look to the sources: does evil reside outside of us or inside? Are we born evil or good? Do we inherit morality? Is it us, the Adversary, or is it God?

So many questions. And while, at the time, given our age and circumstance, they may appear to not be useless, they are in the end, very useless questions. Because in the end, we are what we do and the measure of this is not fixed.

When the inside and the outside meet, that is it. Evaluation, discrimination, all are useless. They are hindrances to clear thought and action.

When I think of myself as a Buddhist, for example, I am far from Buddha. Just as if I think of myself as a Jew or Christian or Muslim, I separate myself from God.

Morality is non-dualistic. It is just being one with the universe in thought, feeling, and action. When we are one with the universe, with no space for judgment, then we are the universe: not good, not bad, not right, not wrong, not pure, not defiled, not born, not dead.

134

Rock, Scissors, Paper

Friday, July 7, 2006

One of the most profound teachings of the Buddha was about overcoming hate. Hatred is one of the three poisons and it is easily spread. Today, we spread hate through our words and deeds, our unkindness, our inability to be present and attentive, our willingness to put whole groups of people into categories barely giving their humanity a nod. We spread hate through our eager willingness to retaliate, as if revenge will pacify our raging hearts. The worst part is that we do this instantly and on a worldwide basis.

The Buddha said that hate only begets hate. Being angry and hateful creates anger and hatefulness in others. And so on. Love begets love. Being loving creates lovingness in others. And I believe this is true, but I also believe this is a very slow and very painful process. There are no quick fixes for hate.

This very slowness of the process is a serious problem in a worldwide community of instant connectivity. Within seconds, pictures of bombings, rocket attacks, police brutality, ethnic and religious violence, wife beating, and so on are sent around the world. We have immediate reactions to these images, we make conclusions about the perpetrators we suffer with the victims and, as victims ourselves, want to not hurt, so we attack back.

Yet we should rather love back. We should listen to the deeper meanings, the pain and suffering of those hateful people who attack us and vilify us, so that we can understand them and their point of view. We see that they and we are essentially the same. We are all beings just trying to survive in a world. When we set aside our hate, we see the needs of our own children and families. When we set aside our hate, we offer love a gate to enter our hearts.

This is very scary because to open ourselves to love means to experience vulnerability. Those who have experienced trauma of the heart and body know this is such a challenge. Yet we know that hate just creates more hate and closed doors wither away our hearts and minds.

To effectively deal with this we must recognize our own impermanence. Regardless of what we do, open or closed, we are not forever. So, in the time we have, how do we really want to live?

135

Losing and Gaining

Saturday, July 8, 2006

A young lady lost her engagement ring in the grass near our courtyard yesterday. She spent hours out there trying to find it. For a while, I searched with her, but the tiny ring was not to be found.

As we searched, she talked about the ring, just receiving it, her happiness, and her panic and hurt over losing it. Yet, she also talked about her fiancé. How he said not to worry, that he will borrow a metal detector to search more deeply for it and if that failed he would just buy her another.

Nothing was really lost. Nothing was really gained. Everything was revealed.

136

The Birds Are Up, The Trees Are Up ...

Sunday, July 9, 2006

Another wonderful morning comes our way. I am listening to the birdsong outside the living room window. The rain we have been having has seemingly made everyone happy. The grass in the courtyard feels more alert, the trees seem taller, and clearly the birds are happy.

Have you noticed that life is like that? Conditions create conditions. When we are surrounded by love and nurturance, we are loving and nurturing; when we are under stress, we are more brittle and anxious. Internal and external coincide.

Yet both sides of this coin lead to our suffering. To be happy and wish for the conditions of happiness are as powerful sources of suffering as stress and anxiety. You say, but wait, shouldn't we be happy? Shouldn't we work to be happy and create the conditions for happiness? I say, of course. In the process though, do not let go of the fact that these conditions are impermanent and will, sooner or later, cease to exist.

This means we can and should properly live only here and now. An eye toward tomorrow, a wink to the past, but fully present now. My sense is that the birds enjoy their day, whatever their day is. And the trees enjoy their day, whatever their day is. They do so because they are completely one with it.

137

Seeking

Monday, July 10, 2006

Enlightenment. Powerful word. Lots of people searching for it, most with only a vague feeling as to what it is. Which creates a question in my mind. If we do not have a clear idea as to what this is, why are we searching for it?

Do we think enlightenment will make us feel better? Think better? Be better people? Will it make us superior to the next person? Will it be a sign that we are somehow special, or that we have finally arrived?

When you come to the practice of Zen, check your motives rather than your enlightenment.

Seeking satori is a big problem. To search means that we are looking. And when we are looking, we are too busy to be present. Stop looking.

138

What's in Your Closet?

Tuesday, July 11, 2006

Someone wrote to me recently asking about pornography and the precept regarding sexual misconduct. The letter was refreshingly candid and clearly presented a picture of a man working hard to understand himself and the precepts.

Internet pornography is a huge mega-billion-dollar industry. This means that a lot of people go to these sites and a lots of women and men participate in conduct that creates the materials for these sites.

The existence of this industry, like prostitution, raises a number of good questions about our nature, ethics, and our biology.

Just what is pornography, anyway? I was sitting in Barnes & Nobles the other day with a friend and her stepdaughter who was 16 going on 21. This young lady picked out a copy of Cosmo, she was wearing a very mini, mini skirt, and was clearly suffering from raging hormones. The cover of the magazine promised information on very specific sexual issues and questions, the pictures in the magazine were tantalizing sexual. What do we make of this?

Is creating or viewing pornography a violation of the precepts? And if so, how?

When does sexual content or conduct become "misconduct"?

I have my own understanding of these questions, but I would like to hear yours.

139

Crickets

Thursday, July 13, 2006

It is a wonderful morning already. I was out with the dogs and relished the cool desert air and feel of the earth under my feet. Crickets, birds, and the gentle swish of leaves as the air moves them: all sounds so delicious getting out early to hear them is worth the effort.

I hear myself hearing them, I see myself seeing them: sky, mountains and my neighbor's windows. Witnessing the witness, know you are they and they are you, the whole universe reveals its true nature.

140

That Pesky Precept

Friday, July 14, 2006

We have brains, hearts, lungs, stomachs, kidneys, penises and/or clitorises. Just as our organs like the brain and heart function without our saying much about it, so too, the others. Yet just so: because the motor is running, it does not mean we must put it in gear and step on the gas.

Second. We live in a natural world. Nothing evil or good exists independent of us. We create evil and good by our actions, and our evaluations of those actions. In the end, it is our intent that creates our karma.

Third. If we are using sexual conduct for health reasons, that is, for improving our mental and emotional states, or reproducing, then our intent is a benefit. If, on the other hand, this behavior is rooted in a desire to harm, to control or punish, then we are using sexuality as a tool for harm and in so doing, creating evil.

Pornography, by itself, as pictures or film, is neutral. It is like the rock under my foot. Or the thought in my head. It means nothing by itself. We add to it with that thought and then create evil or good with our action.

Fourth. The industry of pornography is a whole other matter and thus a matter for us. If we say that smoking is harmful, then those who produce the product we smoke have a role to play in the responsibility equation. When a film portrays violence for the sake of glamorizing violence and thus, promoting violence, it is creating evil. Just so, pornography. We have a responsibility in consuming such material in that sense.

Lastly, life is complex. We are all infants in the process, learning as we go. Sometimes our best efforts at understanding and doing the right thing are either not good enough or, in the worst-case scenario (like a righteous war) short term fixes to long term problems. We should not punish ourselves for our behavior. Rather we should learn from it and do better.

I cannot tell you what better is, only you and your heart and the faces of those you love (or hate) can do that.

141

The Middle East

Saturday, July 15, 2006

May all beings be at peace and be free from suffering. War is not a helpful activity. No joy should be felt in the killing of beings, regardless of the cause.

The Middle East is a place that challenges us all. Deep divisions of culture, time, and faith coexist in increasing conflict and tension. Victims of violence cry and feel angry. Everyone wants to hurt everyone, yet everyone wants everyone else to stop. No one trusts anyone. A place where humanity should shine, a so-called jewel of western religion, birthplace of monotheism and three major religions, and what is there today?

Hell.

Still, it is too easy for us here in the USA to point fingers at one side or the other, and especially at peoples and cultures we do not understand. Aren't we naive to suggest that everyone should just stop all this fighting and learn to get along?

It is not so simple to practice serene reflection in the middle of bombs and rockets, or while people are blowing themselves up calling for the utter destruction of another country. Reason seems pale. Compassion is seriously challenged.

Violence and the threat of violence never curtails violence, just as the death penalty never curtails murder. This is so because violence at its root is not rational and, in its presence, incites additional irrationality in the form of fear. We must work hard to train ourselves to resist fear, to resist catastrophic thinking, and embrace our enemies as best we can by trying to understand them.

How do we accomplish this? We practice zazen. We look deeply within ourselves and embrace our true nature, a nature which we all share, a universal nature. We must each respect each other, agree each other has a right to exist and a place to do so. We must support each other's differences as well as our similarities. It never does any good to only seek the similarities, while pretending the differences don't exist. Those differences then become splinters in our fingers.

Our world is precious, as is each being that inhabits it. Practice this.

142

Matters of Consequence

Sunday, July 16, 2006

The rain came down hard last night. I watched it from my living room as it soaked the ground. It is a real blessing to witness rainfall. Water is so precious. So much of life's preciousness goes unnoticed when we are not present to witness it. We are often not present for such things because our attention is distracted by 'matters of consequence.' And yet, like The Little Prince, we should stay aware that it is the simplest things that are of the deepest consequence.

Rain, a shining sun, the feel of our feet on the ground: these are matters of consequence. The water we drink, the food we eat, the clothes we wear: these are matters of consequence. The love in our life, the hate in our life, and our practice with them: these are matters of consequence.

So, we practice to pay attention. We practice to witness true matters of consequence, allowing our witness to nurture the good and burn away the evil.

This is not difficult. Do it now.

143

Not Always So

Monday, July 17, 2006

When we pray for peace, what are we doing? What does it mean, to "pray" for peace? Prayer is typically thought of as an appeal to God or to a government, or some other such authority.

But this is not always so.

An appeal suggests a disconnect between two or more parties. If we are one, what would prayer be?

I see prayer as less an appeal to others than as a modeling of the thing itself. To pray for peace thus becomes modeling peace. To pray for non-violence becomes modeling non-violence. To pray for the health of others means modeling healthy living. And so on.

When we pray this way, we are expressing the true nature of things.

144

A Candle Against Hate

Tuesday, July 18, 2006

May all beings be free from suffering. A simple prayer, yet so challenging. When people hate us enough to kill us, and do so with glee, it is quite natural to want to kill them first. Natural, but not kind. Natural, but not correct. Natural, but not good enough.

I read a prayer this morning from a religious list that essentially petitioned God to punish our enemies. I was struck by this. It was an opening statement on a ethics text commentary.

When we ask God to take sides, we are our discerning self to take sides. The process of taking sides divides humanity into lumps: those we like, and those we don't like. Simple enough on its surface, but in the end it is very dangerous, as it is very easy to be tempted to see those we don't like as somehow different from us, less than us, or just plain evil.

People who hate are people who suffer. When we pray for an end to suffering, we must pray for an end to hate, especially within ourselves. Hate has a place to germinate when we close ourselves off. Hate loves the darkness of ignorance. It thrives in the shadows.

Today, light a candle specifically for illuminating the dark places of your heart. Place your attention on the light of that small flame. Witness its steady warmth. One small flame, one large light.

145

Being

Wednesday, July 19, 2006

Being in suffering, I walk recklessly. Being in suffering, my attention is on my pain. Being in suffering, I need to escape my pain. Being in suffering I cannot feel for others.

Being at peace, I walk lightly upon the earth. Being at peace, I am mindful of my actions and my speech. Being at peace, love has an opportunity to exist.

Through practice, develop the wisdom and insight to know these are both seeds within each of us and that they are of the same source. Our path is to begin with one and conclude with the other.

146

Take a Bite!

Sunday, July 23, 2006

If we keep a piece of fruit too long without enjoying it, it becomes unenjoyable. Nothing can be saved for very long: the universal processes, revealing the truth of impermanence, cannot be stopped. Yet we try. My, do we try.

Trying to stop change is like refusing the Universal. Here comes the flood, let's stop it! Right!

If we are "lucky" or willing to work hard, we might slow it down, yet in the process, it is interesting to note, we lose touch with that which we are now because our attention is directed toward keeping change from happening.

Enjoy this moment, as it is. If you are exercising, you are enjoying your exercise, not working to forestall a weakened future! If you are eating healthy, enjoy eating healthy, not the thought that you are pushing away cancer or some other dread inevitability.

Take a bite of life and savor it!

147

Freedom

Monday, July 24, 2006

May all beings be free from suffering.

I repeat this short prayer every time I put my palms together in gassho. It is attached to each email post. Like the Tibetan prayer wheel, it is launched by my breath and my touch into the universe.

I recognize that this being, "I", am a suffering being, with all suffering beings. In truth we are one being completely. So to free one being, frees all beings, just as my behavior defines a set of possibilities for all other human beings, and their behavior, mine. There was great and fundamental truth in the basic statements of the existentialists.

Just so, it is not enough to say, we must do. In the doing we are being, never becoming. We are what we do.

So, this morning "do" love, "do" peace, "do" complete oneness.

These things then become realities for us all.

148

Aggression

Monday, July 24, 2006

Aggression will get us nowhere but to the fires of hell. Those who fire the first shot, those who fire the last shot, all will be brothers and sisters there. In times of great pain and suffering we must commit ourselves to great peace and compassion.

Arriving at such a place is a whole other matter.

Along the path of peace and compassion come attempts to stir us. Threats to our well-being, argument, rumor, gossip, people taking advantage of our generosity or our compassion, all of these are serious challenges. Yet we persist.

We persist because we know that our peace and our compassion are not relative, but absolute. They are our true nature. Cultivate this nature. Nurture it. Embrace it.

149

The Middle Way

Tuesday, July 25, 2006

In all things we should live in the middle. Extremes are a serious problem for both religious and secular life, as if the two can really be separated. Cutting off the heads of our enemies, burning a cross in the front of a home, bombing a church or mosque, blowing up centuries old Buddha statues are not the acts of a spiritually based people, but rather the acts of bigots who are essentially spiritual vampires. They live off the life of others.

The Middle Way is neither black nor white. It is not Buddhist, not Christian, not Jewish, not Muslim, not Hindu, not Wicca...it is a way. We practice the Middle way by serene reflection. Allow things to rise and fall away, Doing what is before us to do. Adding as little as possible of ourselves to the mix, we enjoy the moment for what it is.

150

Our Mindful Bell

Tuesday, July 25, 2006

This morning, I felt rushed. I woke late. Without panic, though, I quickly and mindfully got myself to the Zen Center for our morning Zazen. There were three of us this morning and it was delightful to light the candle and offer incense. Reciting the Great Heart of Wisdom Sutra, the words rang like deep bells in my heart and mind. We sat quietly for a thirty-minute period.

At home, I sat down to write to you and Tripper laid down beside me. He is there now, head on my left hand, breathing gently and slowly, completely relaxed. What a warm and wonderful feeling.

In our lives we perceive ourselves moving from place to place, like a boat along a shore. In truth nothing is moving. We are always right where we are. Being awake to this is the real joy of our practice.

We wake to this present moment practice by paying attention to our own bell of mindfulness as it sounds with each beat in our chests.

151

Light and Dark

Thursday, July 27, 2006

As the sun rises, its light illuminates our atmosphere creating our sky and hiding the stars beyond. Therefore, we can say that sometimes the light of day is a hindrance. Truth does not depend on light, it is in itself. Do not be deceived by the light, nor confused by the darkness. Light and dark are but two views of the same reality.

Life requires an open heart and deep faith. Practice being present with both.

152

The Three Treasures

Thursday, July 27, 2006

This morning, I would like to talk a bit about the Three Refuges: Buddha, Dharma, and Sangha. When we "take refuge" in these three treasures we are not going anywhere. Its not like we are entering a cave or a fortress, secluding ourselves from the rest of the universe. These Three Treasures are living and breathing aspects of ourselves.

Each of us is a Buddha, and, in a larger sense, the entire universe is Buddha. It is buddha-nature. Where is there to go that buddha-nature is not? The Buddha himself was only a representation of this, an embodiment, if you will, of us all. Simply a man who through his practice released himself from delusion, freed himself from hatred, and was the pure expression of compassion. When we take refuge in this, we vow to be this.

Each of us is Dharma, and in a larger sense, the entire universe is Dharma. Dharma is the how and the what of everything. When we put this into words, it becomes a teaching, written down it is a scripture. Even in falsehood truth resides.

Each of us is Sangha. Life is not divisible. Categories of life are mental constructions that destroy the wetness of process. All of life is Sangha at various stages of awakening. When we enter the Sangha, we open our eyes to this intimate truth.

Vowing to become one with these is really a recognition that this oneness already exists. In the vow you become a complete expression of this unity.

153

A Six Years Old Roshi

Friday, July 28, 2006

Yesterday through much of the afternoon, I was six years old. I played with a young friend in the pool, we ran in a circle in the courtyard, we played on the floor of the apartment while the adults looked on. We are never too old to see with a child's eye. Our imagination is still a very powerful tool.

I was a Mighty Morphin' Shark, a Bubble Blowin' Jellyfish, and a Floating Log within minutes. And when my little friend had to go home, I became a husband and grandfather again.

These are but roles we play, limited only by our willingness to be ourselves. We can too often allow our limits to encrust us in tradition; age us before our time.

When that happens, go find a six-year-old to play with.

154

They Shoot Jews, Don't They?

Saturday, July 29, 2006

Hate is a powerful poison. It fills us with such negative energy. It demands harmful action and evil behavior. The Buddha said that the antidote to hate was love. Only love will stop hate, yet loving those who would do us harm is so difficult.

Yesterday I had occasion to read several web logs from Muslims. The common theme seemed to be that Jews were not human. Then I read about the man who walked into a Jewish Federation Building, claimed he was a Muslim and shot six people including women.

Sometimes when confronted with such things, I remain silent. I take in the pain of the situation and let it sit with me. Rivers of feeling rush by. Irrational thoughts. Hurtful feelings. I remain silent.

In this silence I begin to understand that point of view is everything. Those who are oppressed, hungry, and powerless will hate those whom they perceive to be well-fed, powerful, and rich. No amount of sharing, goodwill gestures, or outreach will resolve such deep and powerful feelings.

In such cases and in such moments, my prayers must be directed toward myself. Recognizing my anger, I can recognize theirs. Recognizing my hate, I can recognize theirs. Recognizing my suffering, I can recognize theirs. It is through this recognition that our humanity is actualized. For it is true that we can all hate, then it is equally true that we can all love. If it is true that we can all be anger, then it is equally true that we can all be at peace.

So, we begin within ourselves and step outside. Honor your neighbor, love your enemy, and desire peace.

155

And Then There Where None

Sunday, July 30, 2006

Killing is wrong. Enough already. All of the reasons are just words in the wind. Palestine this, Israel that. Men, women, and children die, suffer greatly, and their deaths and suffering become the cause of the next round of bombs and rockets.

We must be better than this. We must be smarter than this. We must have enough courage to live in peace.

Such a challenge, it seems. Forgiveness and compassion for our enemies is so difficult. Perhaps it is really beyond our capabilities. We always done it this way. You throw something at me, I throw something at you. You take this, I take that. It's only human nature, right?

And so the whole world is dead, and no one is left to cry for us. In our graves we will be happy that we were avenged.

How childish.

To live in peace is to live in courage. To live in love is to live in understanding. To live in suffering is to live in compassion. These are the resources we must develop and nurture. These must be our foundation.

156

Create Peace in Your Life

Wednesday, August 2, 2006

We are in Port St. Lucie, Florida and are staying at the Holiday Inn. It is a nice hotel and the weather is wonderful. I have found the humidity at sea level to be a bit uncomfortable but have adjusted by taking it easy. After a long time at the pool swimming and reading...and a rather large meal (Boca Burger and a banana split), I relaxed in bed and went to sleep.

Of course, this means I am now awake early. I downloaded the pictures from our camera, made my "Yahoo 360" note and "Blast." I am about ready to sit Zazen.

Let us all pray that we human beings stop fighting each other. There is so much beauty in the world, so much to do, and so little time to actualize it. It is difficult to build civilizations while destroying others. So difficult to love people when we are killing them.

In all of our actions today, let us be peace.

How difficult is this? For some who are carrying a heavy load of fear and suspicion, it is very difficult. We must each practice Zazen, practice dropping away body and mind, experience the Universe, in order to begin. We must each be that which we most highly value. Model that which we want to see.

I know I still struggle with this. As a human being, feelings and thoughts are tightly bound and rise up like lightning to become behavior. Flashpoints are everywhere, like little minefields. So, we must be vigilant and determined.

With practice my peace is yours, and yours, mine.

157

What to do

Thursday, August 3, 2006

True Bodhisattvas do only that which is before them to do. This is because they live in the real world directly, manifesting themselves in the behavior of the moment. No need to go across the universe when they and the universe are one.

So, as we go through our day, pick up that piece of trash someone dropped on the ground, clean the lint filter of the laundry machine, flush your toilet in the public restroom, wash your hands often, be respectful of what you eat, honor the air you breathe, and offer a stranger your smile.

Make yourself a healing balm against an open wound.

158

Don't Get Stuck In It

Friday, August 4, 2006

How can that which is everything move? Be born? Die? Yet, emptiness becomes form when conditions are correct, then when conditions are no longer correct, form resolves into emptiness. Figure and field are the same, just different; shorthand created by our brain in order to provide a stage for us to walk upon.

When seen clearly there is nothing to see. Don't get stuck in it.

159

Life is in the Details

Saturday, August 5, 2006

We are sitting in the Ft. Lauderdale airport and I thought I would post my morning note while waiting for the aircraft to board. I have been reading closely the Eight Gates of Zen by Daido Loori. It is a rich text, well worth the study.

He said something about liturgy being a method we have in Zen of connecting or actualizing the spiritual with the everyday. He argues that Master Dogen did this when he re-invented the Zen liturgy back in the 13th century.

By liturgy is meant not just the morning and evening services, the sutras, and the vows. But in a much larger sense, the gathas we recite upon opening a sutra, washing our face, shaving our heads, eating, brushing our teeth. Even wider, the mindful attention we place on our every move, thought, feeling, through the day.

To live a Zen life is to live a life awake to the details of the everyday. We know the Universe in those details. And each detail is an opportunity for complete, unexcelled awakening.

160

Being a Buddha

Sunday, August 6, 2006

As we have all read, and some of us practice, to study the Way is to study the self. This has particular meaning for us. It means we must be aware of our responses to the universe as it presents itself. How do we hear our fellow man? How do we read text on a computer screen? What do we add? What do we take away?

Lists such as this offer us a unique practice opportunity. We can take on roles. We can speak from the heart. We can practice deep listening. We can be compassionate. We can be hurtful. Our choices should be our teachers.

Just so in our everyday discourse. Investigating how we interact with our spouse is every bit as important as how we interact with each other in a Zendo, perhaps more.

Being a Buddha is not a part time job, nor is it contained to certain media.

161

Respect

Wednesday, 1ugust 9, 2006

I have spent the last couple of days with the Eihei Shingi, Dogen's work on the rules for monastic life. What I come out of this study with is the sense that respect is key.

Our ability to respect, however, comes only with serious practice. We must be willing to set ourselves aside along with our notions and values, our ideas and beliefs and what we know in order to respect the person in front of us. And we do so simply because he is there.

It is our job to find the Buddha-nature within him, not his job to show us where it is.

162

In the shrill of the night

Friday, August 11, 2006

The world is all a-jitter. Terrorists, terror threats, wars: all before our eyes 24/7. I wonder about the impact of such things on our human psyche. How does one live in constant fear and remain a human being? One doesn't.

The truth is, it's all noise.

An abundance of caution is just a way of justifying giving sway to fear. Caution, good; an abundance, not so good. In an abundance of anything we swim in craziness. Each voice ramping up the next until there's nothing left but the shrill whine of terror itself. We clone each other.

So, here's what to do. Nothing. Doing nothing is always best. Just as there is thunder in silence, so there is peace in vast emptiness. Let the voices rant, be peace in the rage. Smile a lot. Smiling helps. Bow a lot. Humility is always a good thing.

In a placid pond, stones are swallowed whole.

163

Get to Work!

Saturday, August 12, 2006

The world is suffering. Each of us is witness and participant. Yet, what are we really doing about it? From the silence of our deepest practice arises the deepest compassion. How so? Because from our deepest practice comes the deepest realization that everything is one, so that when one suffers all suffer; when one is joyful, all are joyful. When one dies, all die.

Not becoming attached to one state of being or another does not mean ignoring a problem when it presents itself. It does not mean becoming stoic and quiet and withdrawing to the mountains. As Master Dogen points out, even the green mountains walk.

As I sat at the Peace Vigil this past Wednesday, I was heartened by the drivers who honked in our support but was dismayed by the severe lack of people on the line with us. At the Zen Center and at the synagogue I am struck by the lack of attendance. At the soup kitchen, where are the food donations that should be overwhelming the pantry's ability to contain them? At the child care centers and homeless shelters, where are the goods, services, and people that will repair the wounded in our communities?

We are a world of great wealth and great intelligence and yet the distribution of basic necessities, as well as social justice is askew. We are a world now embattled by fundamentalism and the fear that drives it. We see the images and want to turn away.

I say turn away, go ahead! Stop the poison from entering your heart. But then turn to something! You want to reduce suffering? Get to work!

164

The Great Divide

Sunday, August 13, 2006

Offering a stick of incense this morning, I bowed and affirmed that all beings be free from suffering. I say affirmed because all too often when we talk about prayer we are talking as we and the thing we are praying for (and to) are somehow different or apart.

Prayer is not just a request. In its highest form it's an affirmation of non-duality. Just as we resolve a paradox by becoming the paradox, resolve a koan by becoming the koan, so too, we pray.

So, we could say, I pray for peace. Or we could say, I become peace. Or better still, I realize peace. The truest statement is the statement that most reduces the divide between subject and object.

While our language, hardwired in duality, is a tall barrier to our full realization, our practice can be a hammer breaking down that barrier.

Peace.

165

Peace

Monday, August 14, 2006

A fragile peace, and there is no other kind, has been achieved in Lebanon and Israel. How wonderful! Let us all work together to maintain it. Peace is always fragile because life hurts. We don't enjoy suffering and try to stop ourselves from suffering by force. This just increases the suffering of all concerned. A cycle of violence and injury emerges and takes on a life of its own.

To stop it we must find a way to accept the blows of others, verbal or physical, and accept them in such a way as to both survive ourselves and nurture our enemies in the process. Love erodes hatred. It is like anti-toxin. But it is slow working, demanding, and very difficult to produce in the face of hatred.

Still, we must learn this practice. All of us. We must stop taking the violent steps that we take believing they will make us safe and take the far more courageous steps of loving-kindness.

We do this with practice. We do this with love. We do this because we don't have any other choice.

166

Something Wonderful

Tuesday, August 15, 2006

Our window is open and the gardeners are taking a break from their work. It is such a delight to sit here and look out a window onto the courtyard. It is green and there are a few trees. We have picnic tables and tall grasses with even taller plumes. It rained earlier and the air is clean and fresh. I wish you could be here to experience this with me. Yet we each have our own beauty to experience, don't we?

It is so important to stop for a bit and take note of it. In our rush to get here and there, we often miss the simple, natural, beauty that surrounds us. Beauty is everywhere: even in the darkest places. We only need open our eyes and hearts to see and experience it.

Often in the midst of conflict, stress, or suffering of some sort or other, we are so overwhelmed with the difficulty that we just want to close our eyes and make the world go away. Not the best approach, I'm afraid. The world will remain forever. It is our problems that will go away.

What we need to do in such circumstances is work hard to take a moment to see something wonderful there in front of us. Nothing there? Think again. There is always something wonderful. Always.

167

Our Toolbox

Wednesday, August 16, 20006

Have you ever met a person who has had the sense knocked into him?

I have. These people tend to be bitter, resentful, deceitful, and act out of fear.

What is one man's terrorist is another man's liberation fighter. It's all in the point of view. Yet we insist that we can win a war on terror. Hmmm. How should we best go about that? Knock some sense into their heads?

We need to realize that each "war" we seem to engage in (and we love this metaphor for action here in America) requires the appropriate tools. Just as a "war" on hunger does not require Stealth Bombers. A "war" on terror would benefit from a set of tools that might diffuse the terrorist's motivation and support.

So, what motivates a "terrorist"? Ahhh, the problem begins to crystallize. We have no real clue, since we put them all in the same box and mark them up as terrorists. So, this is a one-tool-fits-all war. And the tool is "kill." Rather like that old Arlo Guthrie refrain in Alice's Restaurant, and just so, reveals a level of insanity caused by our unwillingness to talk with people we disagree with or don't understand.

There are lessons for life in this.

Talk with people. Invite them to sit down with you. Listen without packaging up their thoughts before they have left their mouths. Find the commonalities of experience and needs. Be flexible and creative in addressing issues. One tool rarely fits all things. That's why we have soooo many tools.

In the end, it will be our willingness to understand our enemies that will make them our friends. Life is like that.

168

Rain and its Teaching

Thursday, August 17, 2006

We have been receiving rain. Lots of rain. In the desert, rain is both a blessing and a curse. Since it doesn't rain often, the ground is not receptive to the water. The water hits the ground and bounces. Then flows. Then rages through arroyos. We should all learn from this.

The lesson? The ground must be both prepared and willing to receive.

What does this mean for us? We are a lot like that ground. We harden and dry up. We fail to receive in our hardness and defensiveness.

To receive the blessings of a wet world, we must prepare ourselves to be watered. This means we must do the hard work of reflection and examination. We must be willing to dig up the rocks of our past and expose them to the light of day. We must be willing to aerate our soil with dialog. So when the waters of life do visit us, we are both ready and have the space to receive them.

169

Our Nature

Saturday, August 19, 2006

We awoke to a very gentle rain, more a mist really, and it was refreshing to take the dogs outside first thing. I smelled the wet grass and shrubs. I listened to the chatter of birds who have taken residence with us in our complex and stood erect as I took in my breath in silence.

When I opened my eyes this morning, I was listening to the Buddha talk about transformation. My dream suggested transformation was an inside out thing. But I think that is only half right. Transformation is an interactive process requiring all elements to work together.

And just what is transformation anyway? It is simply taking the hook out and letting it go. Pema Chodren talks about being hooked. I enjoyed this metaphor.

We each go through our days encountering situations which distract us from the task at hand. Someone says something. Another reminds us of something. Our jealousy, prejudice, and fear come into play. The hook is sunk into our flesh and we are caught.

Through our practice, we recognize these hooks for what they are and realize we have the skill to remove them.

We do this without much fanfare. It is our simple, but daily work. Just as we recognize our distractions in zazen, then gently go back to our breath in mindful presence, so too, when we take out one of the moment-to-moment hooks, we simply let it go.

We are, as I said, each human and we will be distracted. It is our nature. But it is also our nature to forgive ourselves, nurture our friends and family, and build a loving world.

170

Calm Abiding

Monday, August 21, 2006

The presentation at Unity Church of Mesilla Valley went very well yesterday. We expected 25-35 people. I made 50 handouts. We ran out!

People always seem to enjoy hearing about Zen and the Dharma. They seem to feel calmed by the message. Yet so many resist the practice. My sense is that some people fear letting go of the thoughts and feelings they have, even if they are the causes of their suffering, as those same thoughts and feelings are so very familiar.

The thing is, Zen will not remove thoughts and feelings, nor will it stop pain. It will only alter our relationship to them.

The whole notion of "calm abiding", a phrase often used in Buddhist texts, is about relationship. If we are in a small boat in the middle of a stormy sea, our practice of Zen will not calm the sea. What it will do is calm our relationship to the storm itself. We will do what is natural and necessary to do in order to stay afloat. We will notice the high water. We will notice our fear. We will notice the wind. And we will bucket out the water, take down our sail, and make sure all our things are tied down.

Within the storm and the things to be done, we are calmly abiding.

Now, if we shift our perspective, we see that there is no storm. We see that storm is a word we apply to a set of circumstances and that such a word arouses thoughts and feelings.

So, where is the storm?

Calm abiding is the Zen of relationship to everyday life.

171

What's your message?

Tuesday, August 22, 2006

Consider your every movement, your every words, thoughts and deeds are teachings. What is their essence? If, as was once said, the medium is the message, what is your message?

I see our children wearing t-shirts that suggest they are selfish or sex toys. I see parents not paying attention to much of anything but what's on their table. I see people equating prosperity with election (to use an old Calvinist sort of thought).

Yet this obsession with the pleasures of the self noticeably leaves us feeling both empty and oddly angry. We seek fulfillment (a spiritual sort of meal) in Church or Synagogue or Mosque or Zendo and are angry when we leave still craving. Not understanding that seeking is a sort of sickness in itself. We blame the form or the Teaching or the Teacher. Sometimes we hold the Universe responsible. It is rare that we really get into it, though. Rarely do we look at our own medium and assess our own message.

Perhaps it is time we considered rethinking the notion of looking "the other way" and saw that "way" as our own life.

172

Can You Hear a Pin Drop ?

Thursday, August 24, 2006

My disciple, Rev. Gozen, did his Teisho last night on "Buddhism Lite." Another student of mine, a budding Buddha, asks during mondo period if Zen is not "Buddhism Heavy."

I sat silent.

If the hall is empty, any sound is like a trumpet (Silent Thunder – Mokurei).

173

Mr and Mrs Buttinsky, Our Neighbors

Saturday, August 26, 2006

I went to the synagogue last night. There was a young man on his way to graduate study at a rabbinic school. He gave a talk. Big Mistake. He chose to talk about the Ways of Rebuke. Now, imagine a congregation full of people much older than you and you are telling them how to rebuke their neighbor. Either in one ear and out the other or a rebuke in itself. He could have cast the talk in much more positive terms by suggesting we consider rebuke to be correction or assistance or counsel or whatever, but no. He stuck to the old, archaic term, rebuke...of course, it's a Hebrew word and rabbis, as well as rabbinic students love to talk on the derivations of terms. I can't blame them; I do the same with Zen words. Such talk makes us feel as though we are in the know, you know.

I was struck, however, with the history that rebuking our neighbor is a positive commandment and is considered a good thing to do. This commandment places all of us in a position of being the hall monitors at school, the crossing guards, and the parents of the world around us. It sets us up to be the experts judging our neighbor's behavior and then demands we become buttinskies on top of it! Oy.

Yes, we should approach those who we feel are injuring us or the world. Yes, we should attempt to repair the damage, assist them and ourselves in healing, but rebuke? I'm not so sure.

The Buddha taught that teachings must be specific to the situation and needs of those within the situation. He knew that not all of us are smart, nor are we all artistic or mechanical. Each of us needs to be approached in a careful way, a way appropriate to our ability to understand. This requires a great knowledge of our neighbor. Sadly, few of us bother to get to know our neighbors well enough. And fewer still have the skill to rebuke with care and compassion.

So, I wonder about this commandment and am left thinking it better to address oneself before addressing the flaws of others.

174

Our Mindful Bell

Monday, August 28, 2006

This morning, I am so sleepy. I thought of the story about Suzuki-roshi training himself to literally jump out of bed each morning. Sometimes life is like that. It demands our attention in spite of ourselves. So few of us seem willing to snap to it, though. Our tendencies are to give in to our body's base urges: eat more, sleep more, exercise less, park as close to the store entrance as possible, eat fast foods, anything to avoid doing that which we do not feel like doing. Oh terror.

No wonder others see us as a soft bunch.

One of the qualities of awakened living is having the discipline to be awake. And to be awake means most directly to be present, even if, especially if, we don't want to.

So, maybe that is what we need in our lives, an internal mindful bell that rings and sometimes gently, sometimes demandingly, brings us to attention. But for what?

What is the "so what? " of our practice?

Why be awake when we so naturally wish to be asleep? Fit when we would rather be unfit? Our answer is precisely in the question.

175

Balance as Practice Realization

Tuesday, August 29, 2006

The rain clouds are hanging over us this morning here in the desert and I see it is 66 degrees. I have my running shorts on and am about to go out for a run/walk with the dogs before going to Zen Center for morning zazen.

Going out before the sun rises is a delicious thing. In this way we get to experience the arrival of a new day. Such things are always attended by fresh scents, clean air, and refreshed lines of thought.

I have been considering this whole notion in our culture that we should somehow place our focus on enjoying our lives. While it is a good thing, I am sure, to enjoy our life, we should not want to place that enjoyment in front of other things. What other things?

Well, the suffering of others, the need to take care of our loved ones, the demands of our planet to name a few of the bigger examples. Some things are much larger than we are and when we place our attention on those things it seems our own pleasures diminish in value. On the other hand, to place our attention on increasing the value of our pleasure, we seem to diminish the value of those around us. Those around us become in-service to our pleasure. Not such a good inverse relationship.

The Bodhisattva Way charges us to consider the world first and ourselves second. Yet, as we come to realize through our practice, there is no "world" and "us" difference. So, it is important to use our wonderful minds to attain perspective on such things. Today we call this 'balance.' In another age and with a different slant on it, it would be called 'practice realization.'

176

A Matter of Perspective

Wednesday, August 30, 2006

We are just matter and energy aware of itself. Knowing our beginning, we see no beginning; knowing our end, we see no end.

Because this is so, you and I, my coffee cup and the coffee within it are all one. Because of this, yesterday, today and tomorrow are one. Yet, not always so, to borrow a phrase from Suzuki-roshi.

Always there is awareness. Awareness can be universal or particular depending on where it is placed. Just as when we look at a television screen, the screen occupies the room, but when we look at a photograph of us looking at a television, the television is but a small part of the picture.

As we move through our day, it is good practice to deliberately shift our perspectives of awareness. When angry or intensely joyful, open your awareness perspective. When working in detail, close your perspective. We should practice to do this easily and freely.

And in such practice, our playful, joyful, compassionate Buddha Nature arises.

177

So Much!

Thursday, August 31, 2006

Waking to rain again this morning. This time it is the steady sort of rain that soaks into the ground and offers refreshment to life. I know, still, that this gentle rain could create serious problems though, as the water from the mountains gains speed and comes crashing through the arroyos. When they overflow, we have much flooding.

Local towns have been devastated by such flooding of late.

Too much of a good thing causes as much suffering as too little of that thing. A middle way is the way through suffering. We experience our pain, but not hold it. We experience our love, but do not hold it. Then, like a ship's rudder knows but does not hinder or try to possess the water, we move smoothly through the waters of our lives.

Not everyday can be a day of joy, not every moment can be appreciated. A wise person realizes a value but does not possess it. He guides himself with his priorities and practices but is not mastered by them.

When the floods come, we stay afloat, then do what we can to repair the damage and move on with our lives. Receive everything. Hold nothing.

178

Labor Day

Friday, September 1, 2006

With this weekend comes an opportunity to consider our work. Labor Day weekend has long been a "sale" weekend, a "party" weekend, and a last "family picnic" weekend of the summer. In truth though, most of our holidays are remembrance days. During their passage we should spend some time reflecting on their meaning.

We know that meaning can exist in two ways at least: personal meaning and communal meaning. In each case it is human beings, however, who make the meaning. The communal meaning of Labor Day is often geographic and socioeconomic. If we were living in a heavily unionized city, Labor Day takes on a decidedly different flavor and meaning than say in Miami, Florida where much of the city is devoted to play.

Still, some holidays should have a baseline meaning and this meaning becomes a personal one. The baseline meaning of a holiday is derived from its reason for being established in the first place. Then it is particularized individually and communally.

Labor Day is a day we reflect on the labor it takes to make our lives what they are. For some of us, labor is used as a tool to earn money, for others it is used as a tool to create. Labor involves effort. Labor involves deliberation. Labor involves patience.

Whatever our labor is we should remember it is our labor. To keep it ours we must do it with mindfulness. When we labor mindlessly it loses its value. When we labor for others' sake only, labor becomes an enemy. When we labor only for the money we are paid, money itself becomes an enemy.

Considering labor is important then. A consideration of our labor can enrich our lives by helping us see our relationship to it and to those who do it.

Keeping this relationship, a relationship of mindfulness and compassion, is a very meaningful thing to do.

179

Value

Thursday, September 7, 2006

What is a value? Over the years I have spent being a therapist and now a priest, I have often wondered. My early academic interests were in the areas of philosophy and religion, then social work, which I saw as applied ethics. Core to any 'spiritual' or religious path, is an exploration of values.

A value is a quality we invest with meaning, perhaps. Or perhaps our values are nothing more or less that the named meanings of our lives.

In any event, like all things, value has meaning only when lived, not when thought.

Values that are only thoughtful expressions are window dressing, spiritual candy, or worse: chimera. By thoughtful expressions I mean things we've named and mistaken the name for the thing. For example, when we value peace and do not live peacefully, we are not living authentically. Peace and living peace must be one and manifest in our lives to be a value.

All of our values seem to flow from something, that is they seem to be dependent upon something. In my case, they flow from a single core value: life. So, what supports and nurtures life is good, what doesn't is bad.

In this sense, then, war is a last option, not a first or pre-emptive one. If someone wishes to cause me harm, my resistance to their effort must be measured and only enough to prevent them from harming me. But even before physical resistance, I must emotionally and psychologically resist and attempt to find non-aggressive ways to avoid the conflict in the first place.

Our willingness to do this is a measure of our value.

180

Zazen

Friday, September 8, 2006

Zazen this morning was a quiet affair. I sat alone in the Ino's seat chanting and ringing the bells. Then silence in the upright posture. Zazen is a silent and deeply quieting practice, through the practice periods themselves can be riotous. In the end, just as the breath finds its own rhythm, so do our minds.

I read a piece in Zen Mind, Beginner's Mind a short while ago that caught my attention. Suzuki suggested that talking about the philosophy of Zen was a little blasphemous. He pointed out that talking about what you do not realize is wrong headed. I suggest it is a little like putting the cart before the horse, or like mistaking a picture for a thing.

So, what is Buddhism? Sit zazen!

181

The Real World

Saturday, September 9, 2006

To the untrained student, spiritual practice and practical practice seem to be two different things. Spiritual practice makes us feel good, relaxed, special, closer to the Infinite, whatever; Practical practice encounters the real world and considers its dangers, as well as its needs and benefits. While this may sometimes seem to be so, it is not always so, and in the final analysis, is never so.

When we practice this way, we think we must go to a special place to practice, dress in a special way, take on a special attitude and posture, and so on, in order to be spiritual. Then when we leave that place we can take on the attitude and posture of the real world, thus justifying our need to be unjust, cruel, and self-centered.

Zen does not differentiate between these two worlds. The Master walks in both at the same time, recognizing what needs to be done and doing it, does so with mind like water, thus revealing the truth, that there is only one world.

Buddhist values are practical values. Generosity ends suffering; morality ends harm; patience encourages success; diligence increases endurance; meditation creates receptivity; and wisdom manifests the whole. It is only when we understand what we are doing through the narrow eyes of the self that these seem impractical.

When a stone is tossed into the water, the water embraces it.

182

Cool Air

Sunday, September 10, 2006

It's a nice Sunday morning and the air is wonderfully cool. Summer is clearly coming to a close. The passing seasons can be gentle reminders of the changing nature of things. Change is rarely sudden, though sometimes it can seem so. More often than not, change simply happens in small increments, detectable only when we pay attention.

Zazen teaches us to pay attention. When we practice zazen, we choose to keep our attention focused, our body and mind join together in this focus, and soon, there is nothing but attention.

In this attention resides our True Nature. What is this Nature? Attention itself.

As the sun dims, the flower falls away. The earth receives the petals and the seeds of spring lay in wait. Life is like that. Breathing in, I receive the universe; breathing out, I release myself to the universe. Close attention to these processes reveals everything changes, yet everything is the same.

Then again, sometimes cool air is just cool air.

183

Good Stuff

Monday, September 11, 2006

On this lovely morning, I would like to talk about good things. What are good things? Things that nurture ourselves. Things that we do to nurture others. When you take a few moments to think about it, nurturance is the stuff of life. As plants crave sunlight, water, and soil, we crave activity, nutritional sustenance, and most importantly, love. In my own life, I am often reminded that I do the first two very well, easily actually, but the last one takes work.

Why is it so challenging to love? In the abstract, love is easy. We can say we 'love this' or we 'adore that,' but to actually love it? This takes some work as well as courage.

To love means to undress. It means to let go of our armor and any other sorts of defenses as we allow another to enter our hearts. For those of us injured by ones who cared for us, this can be exceedingly difficult. We want to love, but are at the same time so wary of it. Love becomes an intimacy tango of sorts. We should all take a few minutes a day to offer something to someone else. In the offering, place your thoughts on the person. Open your heart to them. It's a good thing.

Activity is something we all enjoy, well most of us. Some (like me), enjoy solo sports like running (big surprise), others enjoy the team aspect of things.

This does not have to be difficult, nor does it need to be a challenge. Ten minutes here and there through the day. Who doesn't have ten minutes? We each drive and park our cars. So, park far away from the entrance and "walk" to the store. Do walking meditation while slowly pushing the shopping cart at the grocery store. Slowly and mindfully pick up and place items in your cart. Notice how your muscles move, how they operate. Good practice, this. I'm sure with your creative minds you will find other ways to move your bodies!

Nutrition is always a challenge in the United States. Odd, such a wealthy country, yet so poorly fed. Choose a vegetable every day. Choose a piece of fruit every day. Limit your red meat, if you eat such a thing, and your dietary fat. Drink V-8 juice or tomato juice instead of that cup of coffee. Replace a cup of coffee with a cup of green or white tea. Its all a matter of paying attention: being mindful in the everyday.

Lastly and most importantly, practice zazen daily. Establishing a regular sitting time is important, as is making a place to sit. This place should only be used for sitting, if possible. Create an altar for yourself. You might place a photograph or a plant on this alter. Traditionally, Buddhist altars have a candle, a small water offering, a statue of the Buddha, an incense burner and a plant or flower. Again, be creative. Offer yourself a space that is special to you. A space that will nurture you. Then avail yourself of that space and time and just sit.

184

Change

Tuesday, September 12, 2006

Although the sun is already high in the sky, the desert air feels cool. There is a breeze off the mountains, and a lovely scent comes with it. My early morning walk required a long-sleeved shirt and my robe felt comfortable at zazen. All tell-tale signs that we are approaching autumn.

Autumn is a wonderful time. The leaves begin their turn from green to yellow to brown. The dogs are a bit more eager to prance. The birds seem happier. Change is in the air. These are equinox seasons, spring and autumn. They are transitions. Like all periods of change, we can use them to reflect on the past, resist its passing, or look forward to the future, perhaps becoming impatient with the present. Yet, when we do, we miss each moment's particular brilliance.

Being present with change, we see change is really an illusion. Change only exists in our mind as a mental construction. Pictures of what was and compared to the present and yet again compared to what we want the picture to be. The truth is, the present is the only time that really exists for us. And so, what is here now is everything.

Enjoy your universe.

185

Being Present

Wednesday, September 13, 2006

It is late evening as I sit down to write to you. The rain is gently snapping against the pebbles on the ground outside our apartment window and there is an occasional flash of lightning followed by rolls of thunder. It is perfect weather.

Perfection is always about being present. When we are fully present, regardless of what is happening or what we are thinking and feeling, the moment is perfect. How could it be otherwise?

Imperfection is something we add. Perfection, too, is something we add when we think of perfection, imagine perfection, rather than exist completely with the present. The present is always complete. There can be nothing lacking. We might wish there was something else in our present, but this, too, is something we add. Just being in the present moment is enough and complete, and as a result, perfect.

Some of you wondered what I was thinking when I said change was an illusion in an earlier post. Just so, some of you might wonder just what could I mean when I say everything is always perfect. The key is in understanding that our mind is not reality, it is a function of our brain. Our mind creates what we call reality, it puts a color to it, a taste to it, a smell to it, a texture to it, and a thought about it. But the universe is not our mental construction before our mind exists to perceive it.

What is it?

Like that koan about your face before your parents were born, what was it?

Can you be without thought? Before perception? What would be perfect or imperfect there? What would change there?

And now it is no longer raining. Also, perfect.

186

Teaching

Thursday, September 14, 2006

The sound of morning is a deep one. Unseen things are happening in preparation for the emergence of the sun over the mountains in the east. Just as the First Teacher came from the east to the west, so too, our sun casting its light on the world.

Bodhidharma was a curmudgeon. He had a beard. It is said that he sewed his eyelids open and sat in a cave facing the wall with his naked eyes for nine years.

His student, our second patriarch, demonstrated his earnest desire to be taught by cutting off his arm and presenting it to his Master. Finally, the curmudgeon cracked and taught.

Today, we take teaching for granted. Here it is on the Internet, at your community college, at small workshops everywhere. No one jumps through hoops to be admitted. Precious few even see a hoop to pass through. Learning has been studied and teaching has become a profession, just as friendship has become professionalized, the principles of which are now taught in classrooms.

Yet in all of this teaching, something is missing. Something is being overlooked. It is the awesome pregnancy of the moment between teacher and student that comes only with a deep and abiding relationship. We do not support such relationships, professional citizens that we are. We see skills rather than mystery; codified principles, lists of this and that, rather than art.

So even though the sun rises over the mountains, its light is often wasted on those that simply expect it to be there.

Live without expectation and each moment will give birth to itself.

187

Aren't We Special

Friday, September 15, 2006

In our mind's eye, and sometimes if we are not careful, through our practice, we build elaborate, finely crafted necklaces of wisdom. Stunning and beautiful, they glitter in the light of our hearts and minds. Everyone sees our glitter, we ourselves are mesmerized by it. Isn't it wonderful to be so pretty and, well, soooo very special?

Then a low rider pulls up next to us, blaring, thumping base notes pound, tatts and cigarette smoke, profanity, and a stare that chills us. The necklace breaks and all those pretty little jewels fall to the floor.

Our true practice is the practice of being present without any special mantel. Being present even when the present is hurtful, fearful, or smelly we are able to be our fear, our pain, or our offense.

So, what does this practice get us? Nothing. Practice is not about attainment. Practice is about being and that is absolutely all it is about.

So, practice zazen with care. Do not keep your zazen. Do not wear it around your neck as though it were a precious jewel. It is both nothing and everything at once, as are we ourselves.

188

Get a Grip

Tuesday, September 19, 2006

Zen living is an everyday experience. It really does not matter what religion you follow, whether you believe in a God or not, or much of anything else. Zen living is living with an open eye and open heart. Zen living is living with a willingness to be still even when in motion. It is an attitude and a practice. It can become a religion. It can become a philosophy. Yet in either case it is both and neither.

If we commit to a meditation practice and meet our daily commitment, several things will happen. First, you will develop a deep satisfaction over having committed to setting aside time to be with just yourself and your experience of yourself. Second, you Will learn a great deal from this time on the cushion. Third, you will develop the ability to remain present regardless of the experience.

In the end, you learn what you already know. Your time with yourself on your cushion serves as a confirmation of this knowledge. Finally, you discover it is nothing special and yet extraordinary at the same time.

I invite you each to establish a daily meditation practice. It does take a commitment. And a commitment requires something of us. It requires that the commitment must trump our feelings and thoughts. This is the discipline of the practice. For those coming to meditation as a way of feeling good, this is a huge stumbling block because it is those folks who are usually slaves to their emotions and live undisciplined and chaotic lives as a result.

I say to you, get a grip. The reins are yours to hold. Hold them.

189

A Hammer is But One Tool

Wednesday, September 20, 2006

As someone who has spent a lifetime developing a critical mind, I am now spending the rest of my life learning to see it as both a tool and a hindrance. We should each strive to develop our mind. Critical thinking and a sharp wit is important. Knowledge is important. Yet these are not ends in themselves, but rather tools. We must know not only how to use them, but also how not to use them. We must know when to use them and when not to use them.

In spite of what I was once taught, a hammer will not fix the everything. Sometimes a screwdriver, sometimes a chisel, sometimes a pair of pliers: it is not a one tool fits all world.

Zazen can assist us with this. Zazen is being present regardless. It is using discipline to bring our attention to bear without needing to change anything. So if we have reached point "A" that is where we are and we enjoy point A. A thought of point B takes us away from point A. A thought of point B diminishes point B. Enjoy point A.

Wisdom is our ultimate acceptance of the limits of our tools.

190

Accept the Stone

Thursday, September 21, 2006

There is no peace outside of that which we make for ourselves. When we are at peace with ourselves and live in serene reflection, the disturbances of life are just ripples on the pond. Allow the ripples. Accept the stone. No problem.

Our world seems full of pain and suffering. People killing and maiming. People starving. People threatening other people. We might think these are about power and control or money or oil, but I think not. My sense is these are caused by people who suffer greatly. They are victims of their own thoughts and the brains that create them.

When we discover we do not have to be victims, we are free. At that moment of discovery, we realize all of our suffering is created by our mind and its need to have something to do. This is not to say that our pain is not real. If I touch the griddle at Zen Center as I did the other day, it will burn me, as it did. Yet that is not suffering. Suffering occurs when I get caught in a web of thoughts about that incident and the pain surrounding it.

Who do I blame? Why did it happen? Shouldn't something be done to protect me from injury? These are the footprints of suffering.

If we let these thoughts go, attend to the burn, go on with our lives, no suffering.

As the public service announcements suggest, a mind is a terrible thing to waste. Allowing our mind free rein is worse.

Practice zazen today.

191

In the Meantime

Friday, September 22, 2006

Have you ever thought about the phrase, "in the meantime"? Just what does this phrase mean? A mean is a number achieved by adding the universe and dividing the sum by the number of its parts. The mode is the number which occurs most frequently, and the median is the number that is dead center of an array of numbers. In the meantime?

I think it means now. Before the next moment, but after the last. If this is the case, all of our lived time is meantime. We are very casual about this meantime. We see it as something occurring between other matters, often matters of consequence. Yet how is this so? Matters past and matters future are matters immaterial. They are not real. They are constructions.

So, I live in the meantime. The meantime is mine. And like other base things settled at the bottom, those living in the meantime are still within the current. In being nothing special, we are everything that matters.

So, join me in the meantime. Tomorrow and yesterday are fiction.

192

Enough

Saturday, September 23, 2006

Last night we attended New Years' service at Temple Beth-El. The sanctuary was crowded. Everyone was dressed nicely. There was a banquet of sweets in the social hall. And there were armed guards outside the door.

Yesterday's newspaper had a very interesting op-ed piece by Charles Krautheimer. I usually take issue with this conservative, but on this occasion, his words resonated like the bell in the Zendo. He talked about the irony of Muslims protesting with such viciousness statements that suggest their religion was spread through the sword. He noted that monotheism, in general, has a history of such behavior: all of monotheism.

And how can it be otherwise? By definition, monotheists hold one god, praise one god, hail one god. Each slice of the god pie has its supporters, doctors, lawyers, nurses, and soldiers. Each rallying to set their particular understanding above others and in the process...or perhaps to support the process...Denigrating the other two.

We have become such an intolerant species. Our intolerance is everywhere. We are offended by this or that, we are quick to point out what we see as inappropriate and somehow expect the other to learn from this lesson all the while blind to our own biases and cultural ways.

Frankly, at this point in my life, I have little need for such things. I am happy being present. I am happy with the great diversity on our planet. Its richness is so beautiful. Yet the three spoiled children trying to play in the sandbox create a racket any sane person doesn't want to hear.

I wonder whether any god is worth this distraction, this pain, this suffering. Has civilization come to a point where god has become a hindrance to our peace and continued growth?

Zen does not have a point of view. It has only Zen. When we are Zen, mountains are mountains and rivers are rivers. My ice cream is delicious. The mosquito's effort to live stings.

193

Compassion

Sunday, September 24, 2006

As I walk on this earth, so do you. As I sit on this earth, so do you. As I eat, sleep, love and hate, so do you. We are the same, you and I. Just different reflections of Original Mind at work. So, when I suffer, so do you. When you suffer, so do I. Our understanding of each other in each of these gently sweeps away the residue of the illusion we are separate. If we allow it.

Compassion must be voluntary. We allow our feelings to loosen and let go. We allow ourselves to open to others. We become vulnerable, and in that vulnerability, we become the water for the parched plant.

It is not easy to be so vulnerable. Vulnerability demands of us. It requires we actively address those things that would harm us. So that we might continue to enjoy our vulnerability and nurture others. Addressing harm, however, without protection, requires a willingness to experience pain.

This is why compassion is courage in another form.

Frankly, I am not so good with this. Perhaps I am a coward. It is so difficult for me to not protect myself. I do not want to feel the pain of you, nor my own. I sometimes want to be on a mountain, aloof, apart, untouched and untouchable by you.

Yet here we are. I am down off the mountain. Not such a small thing.

So, while vulnerability is a choice, and our willingness to be with another is salve to injury, and we are born with them, life can often harden us and make it difficult to be the buddhas we are. We can take small steps. We can feel each other's pain. We can learn to enfold that pain with our love and make it better.

I believe this. I believe this very deeply.

194

The Great Teacher

Monday, September 25, 2006

The desert air is cool. I am sitting by the living room window and feeling a chill from its touch on my shoulder through the open window. The feel of natural air, unconditioned by our machines, is a delight. The less we process things, it seems, the better they are.

So too with zazen.

When we sit down on our cushion. We should just sit down, back upright, shoulders open, and head erect. We feel the bones as they seem to organized themselves one on top of another while taking our seat. There is nothing special about this save the deliberate nature of being still. Nothing conditioned. No machine involved. There is just zazen.

We should not process this experience while in the experience. Processing things takes us away from them and in fact, kills the moment. Being witness with a student's eye is being there without a self. A student's eye is unencumbered by the dust of "things we know."

Practicing this way is the great teacher.

195

Boxes

Tuesday, September 26, 2006

The other day someone said to me they "had enough religion." That comment, meant to be an offhand reply about coming back again to a service, has stuck with me. Like one of those scriptural phrases or a line of poetry, it rolls around in my mind.

A comment like this suggests religion exists outside of us. I suppose for some this is true, they slice life into pieces and create boxes: this is spiritual, that is religious, this is philosophical, that is scientific, and so on.

Actually, we all do this. It is an aspect of our mind, created by our brain, that we do it. And like any organ, it functions autonomically. What do we do with the products of such production?

Some of us take these products seriously, see the slice as existing outside of us, as if we were simply remarking on the natural state of the universe. We fail to see how silently and how quickly our mental knife cuts, sorts, and moves on. In fact, we fail to see we are doing it at all.

So, we live in a world of boxes. Some ours, some others. Comparing, valuing, and selecting, boxes and symphonies of boxes compete. We work for this box, we've had enough of that box. We love this other box and hate that one over there. All the while not understanding that the boxes are our own mental creation and that actually there are no boxes, just life.

Our practice is the practice of living without boxes. Everything is us. Nothing is not us.

196

The Thirty Second Zen Master

Wednesday, September 27, 2006

Our practice is not talking practice, it's not philosophy practice, it's practice practice. Zazen is something we all would like to do. Many people want to meditate. Few do.

Everything is a problem. Not enough time. Our back hurts. Our legs hurt. It's too noisy. There is nowhere in our homes that we feel comfortable. Our spouses aren't supportive. We have children, dogs, cats, jobs... you get the idea.

All of these, however, are not problems. They are real opportunities. Zazen is not outward, it is inward. Zazen is about our attitude: right understanding. When our understanding is correct, then everything becomes zazen.

So, what is correct understanding? When we are completely present with ourselves and our activity. When the map, compass, body, and mind are in complete alignment, that is right understanding. With this understanding every step is the correct step, naturally.

We attain correct understanding, however, through our practice of seated meditation and mindfulness.

Therefore, it is important to find five minutes to be still. Five minutes to place your attention on yourself and your environment as if you were simply there as a witness. Five minutes of serene reflection. If not five minutes, then one minute. If not for one minute, then thirty seconds. Become a 30 second master!

It's rather like prayer, you know, No need for a fancy church or synagogue or mosque. No need for a priest, minister, or rabbi. No need for an official time, public pronouncement, advertisement of any sort. Just do it.

197

Grandparent Zen

Friday, September 29, 2006

In Memphis, we are enjoying Baby Tate immensely. He is nothing but cute, inquisitive energy stuffed into New Skin with eyes and fingers, mouth and feet.

Our practice is being witness, guide, protector, clown, and nurturer.

I've exchanged my morning zazen for a kindergarten of one. We learn to make cereal bowls into bells, Cheerios into offerings, and dirty diapers, incense.

This is the Way of Grandparents.

198

A Single Step

Saturday, September 30, 2006

There are always moments when we don't feel like doing what we are supposed to do. Small Mind whispers, "do it later, it'll be OK." Or, "you shouldn't have to do anything you don't want to do." Or, "it's just one day, it won't matter."

These are the whispers which take us away from enlightened living. They help us keep our eyes closed. They keep us slothful, lazy, and ignorant.

Enlightened living is immediate, direct, diligent, and vigorous. We do because it is ours to do. And the whole universe is us so everything is our responsibility. So what is it we should do?

Understand a leader is by definition alone. Because you are there by yourself does not mean you are not making a difference. Become informed. The world needs informed individuals. Be willing to act. The world needs engaged human beings. Become fearless. The world needs people unafraid of what others might think. Become enlightened. The world needs decisive, non-wobbling Bodhisattva Warriors. The step is yours to take.

199

A moment in Time

Sunday, October 1, 2006

This morning I woke late. Our visits to Memphis to see Grandson Tate are real vacations. I have set up a small altar in my daughter's walk-in closet. I brought cedar incense, my zafu, and a small bell. I sit there for a period in the evening before bed.

Morning Zazen is out. At least a formal period. Too many people with differing agendas. So, I sit for small moments. As we talk, play with the baby, wait for dinner, or some other activity. I bring my back up, plant my feet like small trees, and sit still. The moment and me join hands.

In this way we can be mindful throughout the day. Taking every sound and scent, taste, and action, as a temple bell. Such moments are delicious. Yet we should never become attached to them. The most important thing is what we do with our mind in each moment. If we use our mind to cling, to add value, diminish value, or in other ways distort the moment, big problem.

Better is to just be.

And so it goes.

200

Atonement

Monday, October 2, 2006

All my past and harmful karma,
born from beginningless greed, hate, and delusion,
through body, speech, and mind,
I now fully avow.

(From the new Soto Shu translation of the San Ge Mon, the Verse of Repentance)

For Zen Buddhists, these words have particular meaning. They speak to our understanding of the deep and intricate interconnection of everything, past, present, future, cause, effect, and release.

Each morning we recite this verse, knowing that our behavior is most important. Our behavior creates good. Our behavior creates bad. These behaviors are remembered by ourselves and others. Good and bad are conditions within which other things grow, both good and bad. When we do harm, harm is added; when we do something healthy, health is added. We see in each the possibility of evil and the possibility of good.

So, we acknowledge these do not exist apart from us; they are us. No devil, no god, just us. Confronting this truth is very difficult as it requires us to understand thoroughly that everything is ultimately our responsibility. Everything.

We could say that our current bad attitude is a result of our parents, thus we live in their bad karma. This would be true. Yet, when we look deeply into our own nature and see our True Self, the self that existed before our parents were born and will be in our great, great grandchildren, as well, we see this is also false. There is no parent, no child, no past, no future. Just the minute-to-minute manifestation of Buddha nature.

OK, so we inherit, and we plant. What we do with what we inherit is ours and what we plant is ours. Some of us are unaware of this fact. Some of us live in delusion, believing there is a god and a devil who are apart from us and that the world is thus divided. As Bodhisattvas it is our commitment to assist them, to help them, guide them, to see the light of non-duality.

This simple verse allows us to keep in mind precisely where we fit, that is, dead center, in the universe. Each of us, small universes reflecting each other, yet deeply interactive.

The last line of the verse is crucial: I now fully avow. We do not use such words today in everyday discourse. Perhaps we should. According to American Heritage Dictionary, to avow means

To acknowledge openly, boldly, and unashamedly; confess: avow guilt. or 2. To state positively.

I would rather understand "guilt" as "responsible" but guilt is also true. We moderns don't like to think of ourselves as guilty of much of anything, we'd rather feel responsible, as if there were a difference. Either way, to avow is to acknowledge our part in what we have created, good bad or indifferent, and to do so boldly, directly, and without flinching.

In contemporary times, we promote the notion that we are OK. We like to think that our behavior is not all that important, certainly not as bad as someone else's. When we are caught we immediately shift responsibility to others. In this way we seem like Teflon. Nothing sticks to us, we think. Yet this is an illusion as well as a serious flaw in our character and a shortcoming of perception.

Moreover, it also takes us away from our humanity, for to be human means to be self-aware and self-awareness carries acknowledgment of responsibility. In the end, this short verse brings us home to ourselves, it wraps us in our humanity like a warm blanket and offers us a way to become better human beings.

What will we do with our awareness? What will we do with our responsibility? This choice is ours and ours alone. Choose wisely.

201

When Dark Encounters Light

Wednesday, October 4, 2006

The recent horror of the killing of school children in Amish country has offered us a teaching on the darker side of dependent co-arising. We see immediately as it happens, the activities of people across the globe: bombings in the Middle East, shootings in Europe and America, starvation in Africa. We feel in response. We fantasize in response. We establish a point of view in response. So, when we go outside each day, this response is our understanding. We behave accordingly.

Communication can be a valuable tool. Interactivity can be a golden opportunity to deepen our understanding. Yet each can also drive us into despair and create chains of toxicity that enslave us to our more base emotions.

We must counterbalance these offerings from the communication network with other practices. We must practice deep listening. We must practice stillness. We must open ourselves to this pain so that none of us suffer. An open wound contains nothing in itself. An open wound can flow freely and clean itself. Close the wound prematurely and we capture toxicity, allowing it to hide and fester. The pain from a hidden wound can be surprisingly challenging.

So, this happens because that happens. When a bad thing happens, notice. Then open yourself to your feelings about it and let yourself flow some.

Then offer yourself an opportunity to understand, contextualize, and grow from the experience. And in all of this, if you know that your purpose is to be in service to others, your experience of the suffering of others offers you a starting point.

202

Your Own Authority

Thursday, October 5, 2006

Yesterday during an interview with a student, I tried to teach something about walking in one's own authority. This is such a challenging notion. It does not mean being full of oneself. Nor does it mean being a dictator. People who walk in their own authority are confident in themselves and as a result of that confidence have little real need for the signs and symbols of their authority.

When we make ourselves in the world, we should do so simply and directly. The plan and the activity of building should be seamless, as if they were what they are: one.

There is a spin on one of the Dharma seals, "shoho jisso", which means all things are themselves ultimate reality. This is another way of saying "it is what it is" and adding everything is truth.

When I open my eyes and take my breath, I express my true nature. As I pour my coffee, put on my clothes, walk my dogs, I express my true nature. No need to be anything, I am what I am. When we live this way we are living within our own authority. And this is important because it is authentic.

So many of us live in fear of the thoughts and judgments of both others and our inner self. Our choices are the result of an internal dialogue rather than a direct expression of our being. So, what is it, after all, that we fear? Why the chatter? Why the wobble?

If you are going to light that match, light it. If you are going to strike that bell, strike it. If you are disabled, be what you are. No need to hide or get permission to come out.

Our practice is simple, yet so challenging. To be upright on a cushion and live there directly in the moment. Once our mind thoroughly understands there is no threat, no problem. It releases its grip, lets go of the rudder and allows us to be what we are.

203

Holding On

Friday, October 6, 2006

We only see things as coming or going when we live as if we are the reference point. Zen practice enables us to realize this is not always so and, in fact, there is no reference point. With no self as a point of reference, we are free. At that moment, coming and going cease, as do up and down, and most importantly, birth and death.

Our brain produces the ability to link things and events together. Yet in truth, things and events are not linked. They are discreet moments unto themselves. It is only our mind that puts them together as a pattern. While patterns can be delightful and meaningful in the everyday world of relative existence, they are illusions of our mind and should only be understood as mental tools. If we understand them to be truth, we are lost.

To be lost means to not be able to live directly as each thing presents itself. When we live in a pattern we are living in a mental connection and so cannot appreciate things as it is; thusness.

So, challenging for us as ordinary people. But when we practice zazen, we are not ordinary and we begin to see clearly perhaps for the first time. This is the frightening aspect of zazen. It demands that we let go of the post that holds us tethered. As we practice we begin to see the post, the tether, and that which is tethered as illusion, and not entirely there yet, we become frightened.

What will happen to me if I let go?

204

Bodhidharma Day

Saturday, October 7, 2006

Today we celebrate Bodhidharma Day in Las Cruces by being in mindful practice at Zen Center. Bodhidharma was a simple monk who came from India to China in the late fifth century. He taught simply, but consistently, that zazen was the core of the Buddha's teaching. He was a pragmatic and experiential sort who lived in a cave and gazed at its wall. No fancy temples, no fancy clothes, just his body and a wall with a strong determined practice. We consider this man to be the First Zen Patriarch. All current Zen lineages call him parent.

If you are nearby the Zen Center today and would like to sit in stillness for a while, please feel free to join us.

Last night some friends gathered at a local ice cream stand:

Eating ice cream in the wind,
Chocolate drops on a field of blue;
The moon is bright in the sky.

205

The Hard Work

Sunday, October 8, 2006

Everything is as it is and should be. Oh my. What a statement. I hate this! I love that! I vow to cease doing evil. I vow to do good. Yet all are dharma, all are empty of substance, permanence and independence.

When we say good karma or bad karma, we are adding something to cause and effect, a moral judgment, Karma is not about good or bad. Karma is just the process of action.

The hard work is not becoming attached to either. I say hard because we usually understand attachment to mean something like sticking to something of value. To not stick is not to say we don't value. Nor does it mean that we cannot attempt to stop bad from happening. It's like that other sticky wicket word in our vocabulary, acceptance. Accepting and, its emotional action equivalent, 'letting go,' do not imply behavior, but rather refer to an attitudinal position we take relative to what is there before us.

Attachment really points to our contemporary understanding of emotional investment. The more we are emotionally invested in an outcome or object of our desire, the more we suffer as that object eludes or escapes us. Lower the emotional investment, lower the suffering. The object of our desire and our action to achieve it remains, but our suffering in relation to it ends. This is a very important point.

We can love, hate, and value without investing our being in the objects of these. Accomplishing this is the true work of our practice.

206

Almost Odd

Monday, October 9, 2006

Waking to rolling thunder and a wet breeze I am reminded of jungles and the scent of fear. It's odd how one thing recalls another, but I believe this is how our mind works: a sort of memory karmic action.

Yesterday, I had an occasion to meet an elder writer. At 98 she has come out with a memoir. She is a delightful woman and sat gracefully in a chair signing her book. I sat next to her for a while. On my other shoulder was a man I had met elsewhere. A Vietnam combat vet, like myself, who still cannot sleep and still is haunted by decades old demons.

We talked.

Both people had memories, both said they wished some of their memories would disappear, yet one uses her memories to contextualize her life; the other finds memory a felonious intrusion.

As I sat between them, I remembered a return trip to Vietnam I took with my wife and some other Vietnam Vets some years ago. I recalled sitting at a long table in a dining room in some humid northern province. One side, an array of American Vietnam veterans; the other side, an array of North

Vietnamese Army veterans. We traded shots, this time however, the shots were not metal, but rather cheap Russian vodka.

We shared stories and photographs, we laughed and cried. Just a mess of sloppy human beings discovering our ability to forgive and embrace. I noticed as I told this story, my veteran friend withdrew and responded with a slight degree of fear. I think it is this that so deeply separates us.

Today I sat in a beautiful living room with a group of talented writers, eating petit fours and sipping punch. Almost odd, but so distinctly human.

Fear is a clear hindrance in our mind. If allowed, it drives us into caves of darkness wherein every shadow is a killer. Yet I know it is possible to be like a small candle. Still, and serene illuminating without blazing, teaching ourselves that the monsters we fear are only ourselves in darkness.

207

What's In Your Moment?

Tuesday, October 10, 2006

On a mountain, in a desert, on a plain, in a meadow, in the rain, in the sun, in the dark, in the wind: just be there. We do ourselves such a disservice always being somewhere else. We seem to think there and here are different. I suppose they are, in a manner of speaking. Yet, fundamentally, they are the same, earth, sea, sky and the face of human construct. When we appreciate somewhere else more than somewhere here, we are never really here and here itself seems the fiction.

Reality is never tasted this way. We live in a dream. Until the snap of lightning or the dropping of a glass to bring us to the present. Ah, the cocoons we are able to create! So pleasant.

We say, "I take refuge...together with all beings..." reminding us that living in the truth of the here and now is living in a world without duality. It is nowhere special and hardly distinguished. It is just here. This little finger touching this little key touching your eye and thus, your mind, and noticing this fact without much ado.

We practice zazen to appreciate this moment as fully and completely as possible, and then the next. We practice zazen to help us stay awake, that is, present, and nothing more. Knowing that living in this small thing is everything.

208

Change

Wednesday, October 11, 2006

Human beings are builders. It's what we do. We build houses, social structures, spiritual structures, and connections so that these structures come together and live. In this sense we are alive and enable life. When we break down the connections, the energy flow is broken and the parts begin to fail. We call this entropy.

So what happens when as individuals we retire from building?

Another way of understanding this is in terms of meaning building. We create meaning in our lives and meaning is so important that its absence can threaten our very existence. So, when do we stop creating meaning?

Retirement is death.

We human beings must evolve. We must throw away such notions as retirement. Instead, it would be more useful, and healthy, to think of it as exploring. At various stages of our lives we explore and build in various sets of areas: education, work, relationships, family, community, church, temple, or mosque. As we age, we move from one set of interests and areas to others, each time exploring, filling out, adding, deleting, and so on. My sense is that this process is eternal.

Some of us, though, seem to stop. We get tired. We no longer are interested in the world. And then we dry up and die and are scattered about the ground. And even in this are building.

It must be noted that it is in fact only a seeming pause. This pause is another transition allowing us to become material for the next generation. It is only our hubris or fear that refuses to allow us to see this clearly.

209

Being Good

Friday, October 13, 2006

We live to be good people. Yet sometimes, I think we slip into just living, not even just living, but a sort of existing that includes going through the motions of eating, talking, working, sleeping, with no attention on what each moment of being is for us.

How do we live to be good people? What is required of us? Do we need to be superheroes? Heroes? Do we need to be Great Buddhas? Jesus? Moses? The Prophet?

When we walk along the sidewalk, we notice an ant and step over the ant. When we notice there is no toilet paper on the roll, we replace the toilet paper. If someone is angry with us, we listen. If someone needs us, we are there. These are nothing really special, nothing extraordinary, yet so often we are so asleep that we step on the ant, leave the bathroom, blow off someone's feelings, and turn on the TV. Modern life has many exits.

Being present has only one: zazen. Zazen is the practice of being present. Attention to the world within us and without us: we are neither engaged nor disengaged. Whatever is there is there and we are with it 100%. Our body is upright; our mind is upright; our heart is open. Practice.

210

Religious Life

Saturday, October 14, 2006

This morning, I woke to a gentle rain. How nice to hear the tender sound of raindrops. My Little Honey is already out the door. She and friend Deana are attending some yarn or knitting event. They hope to sell buttons they have made. So, I am home alone on a Saturday morning. A day of rest. No Zen Center. Just myself and the universe. Well, there is Tripper, who tries to eat Pete-kitty, who will have none of it, and of course, Pepper who just watches all the fuss.

I must say I do enjoy this stage of my life, enjoying such moments as this. Zazen has taught my body/mind to accept the moment without very much conflict. Conflicts that do arise are settled quickly because they are there to be resolved. Arguments are less hostile, more pliable, and end quickly.

This is being upright. A duck on water, choppy or still, is a duck on water.

The rain is increasing its tempo. We have gone from waltz to four-step. Perhaps we will be witness to a tango. It's just rain. I sit under the canopy of my apartment, participant-witness to it all.

This is religious life.

211

The So What Practice of Zen

Sunday, October 15, 2006

We have all heard the phrase, "no time like the present." In Zen this is considered a daily mantra. Past and future are creations of mind. Yet we must be careful not to make the present moment a creation as well.

We live in the present by living directly, mindfully, and without the craziness that comes with discrimination. Here in this moment, there are plastic keys. Fingers. Electricity. Light. Yet, as soon as I name these, they are not it at all. Now they are my language applied to the phenomenon. What is light before we call it light? What is plastic, finger? Before the two meet?

Who cares.

When the light is on, appreciate it. When it is time to write, write; time to clean, clean. This is the "so what" practice of Zen.

Living in the past, we are dead. Living in the future, not yet born. The present is not a theory. It is what it is: appreciate it.

212

Sangha

Monday, October 16, 2006

Sangha, the last of the Three Treasures, is most likely the most challenging for us in the United States. Not only are we an ego-centric and ethnocentric lot, but we have so little sense of real community. If we sit zazen and the self does, indeed, fall away, what do we have to support us? Our Lexus? Our salary? Our favorite television show?

We are not a people that put ourselves out for the sake of the group. In fact, I suspect, we compete with and against the group in order to gain advantage in our hierarchical position within the group. Oh my.

And so, what is Sangha?

Typically we think of Sangha as a "community" of like-minded individuals who have gathered together for mutual support in their practice. In olden times it was a gathering of monks. Today, its about anyone even to the vastness of all sentient beings. Way too large for me, that is. I like to know my group. I like to see them, smell them, touch them. I like to know they are human beings. That they eat, fart, and make mistakes. I like to know that they are willing to grow, to suck it up, to change. It's important that they be present when I am in need, and I am present when they are in need. Yet this cannot happen when we do not share.

Is it so challenging to unzip and step out of the jackets of our everyday existence? Is it so difficult to be known? To be vulnerable?

I suppose today it is and thus the challenge of Sangha. To take refuge in this treasure is one of the most difficult as it requires a level of trust that we don't ordinarily allow ourselves to have. Sometimes it will be abused. Sometimes there will be no one there to catch us as we fall and we will strike the floor. This should not matter. We are what we choose to be, regardless of the behavior of others.

To make Sangha work we must be Sangha from the inside out.

Consider this when you engage with someone or not engage with someone. In the end it is only your heart that matters, knowing that your heart is the heart of being.

213

What it is

Tuesday, October 17, 2006

When we truly understand everything is relative to everything, then we see nothing is anything more or less than anything else. And when we stand on a single point, everything is relative to it. Where do we stand?

I prefer not to. But, unlike that fictional scrivener, Bartleby, I will be what is there to do.

It has taken a long time to get to this place. I highly recommend it. The mountains are what they are; the rivers and, in my case, the desert, is what it is. And then it is not. Being comfortable with the flow of process is key to our survival and ability to see clearly. Those looking for solid ground, even for an instant, are consumed by the rivers that run through them.

214

Cease Doing Evil

Wednesday, October 18, 2006

The first of the Three Pure Precepts is "Cease doing evil." Not so simple in today's world. What, after all, is evil? Evil conjures up all sorts of things, the least of which is Halloween masks or Tales From the Crypt. Evil is something we too often see as very specific. War. Violence. Cruelty. Evil has a face we believe and more, a face we are all apt to both see and agree upon.

I'm not so sure. I suspect the true face of evil is much more subtle and difficult to see.

Evil causes harm, it erodes life, kills, causes us to suffer. But, then, so does good. Choosing even in the affirmative always negates something. Perhaps it isn't the actual choice so much as choice itself? To choose one person over another for a transplant. One country over another for our aid. One battle instead of another. Or not to fight at all. So what is evil? That which causes harm? Every day we cause harm. Is it a matter of scale? Or intent? Or consequence?

Is it enough to be aware? Enough to translate that awareness into some sort of action?

I don't know.

I think my questions are important, terribly important. I think we do not think about them nearly enough and should talk about them often. We certainly don't pay much attention to them as we live out our daily lives. But, on the other hand, that's why we practice zazen, isn't it? To raise our level of awareness? To get mind, body, and environment in sync and on the same page?

215

Picky, Picky, Picky

Friday, October 20, 2006

This morning at Zen Center I was accompanied by one other: faithful to Zen too. We sat together and we witnessed the wonderful bird song. The Zen Center was chilly. It is cool. And after our incense offering, I made pancakes and eggs with hot coffee.

My griddle was a tad too hot, and I forgot to put some oil under the eggs, but other than that, the food was perfect.

In Zen we have a saying that we should accept what is offered. Of course, we are not to take what is not offered either. Both of these suggest we set ourselves, desires, tastes, and other discriminations aside.

So, when the pancakes are a bit dark and hard and the eggs aren't exactly over medium, well, we eat and enjoy and thank the many lives and hands that brought us the food.

I struggle with this on occasion, picky eater that I am. I don't want a lot of fat and sugar in my diet. With so many people starving to death in our world, how can I be so picky? On the other hand, I prefer vegetables and fruits, love nuts and cheese, and eat cherry tomatoes like candy. Still, I rarely make demands on wait staff, complain about my food (except to My Little Honey), and otherwise allow my feelings to rule my life.

Please consider making a generous offering to your local food pantry today. And in the process, remind yourself there are millions of others who cannot afford to pick and choose.

216

Relative Certainty

Saturday, October 21, 2006

Zen always has a person by the hair, short or otherwise, and yanks them about. Everything is relative to everything else, form has no substance, everything is in flux, we teach; yet 'no substance' takes form, in the flux there is some 'thing' and there is an absolute. In Zen, context and method are everything.

To say something, anything, is always incorrect because words are pale pictures of actual experience. We say behavior reveals our understanding. Much like a flower reveals the soil.

People can catch themselves on hooks of their own making. Waving in the wind as a fish flopping about out of water, we create much ado with our words. And so our great ancestors often cite: silence is thunder.

On the other hand, words are one of the major conveyances of our thoughts and feelings. Silence may speak volumes but is always open to complete misunderstanding. Of course, a true Master could care less and would only see this misadventure as a teaching opportunity.

Care should always be taken with our speech and we should never be so certain about the truth we think we possess. Sometimes silence is thunder, sometimes its just an invitation. When we understand form is emptiness, we should immediately understand emptiness is form. The relative only makes sense in the backdrop of an absolute.

217

On Being a Duck and
Other Matters of Consequence

Sunday, October 22, 2006

There are always moments when we are not ourselves. Lately, I have been experiencing many such moments. My practice is good and it is steady. Still, the ordinary breeze that provides movement for my life has sometimes become a tornado.

Recently we have decided to sell our mountain Refuge. We have talked about moving to Memphis. Lots of serious and radical changes seem to be setting off cascades of feelings. Uncertainty, loss, all those yucky sorts of things burble around.

During such times I sense it is important to be many things at once: open, calm, flexible, and yet centered. Of course, this isn't always possible and sometimes I feel somewhat hypocritical when I flame up and get angry, sullen or withdrawn.

I think, "I should be able to handle this!" All the while festering inside, my duck rocking around on choppy seas.

In this stage of my life it is so important that I have family: my wife, my children and grandchildren. I need a home. Yet life isn't really like that, is it? Life is fluid. Evolving, undulating, washing up here, fading out there. What's a good duck to do?

We could say, "float". And I suppose this is the best answer, yet it clearly is lacking, since direction always seems important. Even old Zen Masters like Dogen suggest this. In his Tenzo Kyokun, he says we should prepare tomorrow's meal this evening, but while doing so, we should be completely present.

So, here it is. I have no idea. My present is, my tomorrow may be something else again. Uncertainty seems to be my foundation.

All we can do is the best we can in each moment we are awake.

218

Oh, Emotion!

Monday, October 23, 2006

When we are afraid and are willing to remain in the fear we can learn. It is the same with anger, joy and sadness. Our feelings can be understood as gates which open to our heart-mind. Care must be taken, but it is best if the gates remain open.

When I am afraid, I tend to seek defenses. Of course, it's also a good idea to turn on the light! And often, once the light is on, there is no longer anything there to fear. So, fear is often about not-knowing. If I am afraid and do not turn on a light to look at what is there, I am likely to build a fortress around me with attitude, feelings and words that are enough to scare the bejeezus out of an elephant. Much simpler to turn on a light. Simpler, but all too often, more challenging.

What is it we are so afraid of? Our unwillingness to be vulnerable speaks volumes about us, doesn't it? In the end, what will happen will happen...or already has...not-knowing and staying in a fortress in the dark will not help for long.

Turning in the light means being willing to be still with yourself in the midst of whatever is happening around you or within you. When we lose our stillness and succumb to the waves, we only need to turn our attention to our breath and the experience of the moment, be it anger, fear, sadness, or joy. These feelings are not lethal, they are feelings, they will always fade away.

Yet, as a group we are woefully inadequate at dealing with them when they are there. Even our emotional vocabulary is poverty stricken. And without a word, we cannot create a sense of mastery. It's as if the parts are just 'out there' buffeting us about the head and shoulders. We say we 'hate' this when we mean we don't like it. We feel 'enraged' when we actually feel annoyed. We are emotional hyperboles.

This tendency is very dangerous as feelings are the drivers of behavior. Too few of us learn how to push in the clutch. And we are off!

Zazen is an excellent practice for learning about the clutch. I recommend it.

219

Meaning

Tuesday, October 24, 2006

Meaning

Waking this morning
to a gentle rain against the window
The sound was nourishing.

Inside, under the cover of the patchwork quilt my wife made,
safe and cozy,
able to perceive the sound of the rain.

Outside, a different matter altogether.
No safety, no warmth.
Just cold wet water.

The rain is the same.

220

Of Our Own Making

Wednesday, October 25, 2006

Of Our Own Making

When the sky is so beautiful
I fail to see the gentle grass.

Big Mind is so seductive.
I want to smack it.

That grass is home to snakes,
Yet it frames the sky.

Little Mind is so ordinary.
I want to puff it up.

Every picture needs a frame,
Every frame, a picture.

I am a metronome:
both artist and audience.

221

Life Is Like That

Thursday, October 26, 2006

The challenge of serene reflection meditation is rather steep. On the surface it appears very easy, just sit still for a while. Yet, when we make the choice to stop our movement, things seem to happen: an old pain surfaces, an itch develops, an awful thought arises...or a very pleasant one. So just sitting there itself becomes a serious obstacle to what we want, namely, to move.

I recommend not moving.

Serene reflection meditation is not relaxation, nor is it a means of finding bliss. It is not therapeutic and it is not easy. It is hard work requiring your constant attention.

Life is like that.

When we practice living we tend to think of it as easy. Oh, if I were twenty-one, no problem! If only I had a better job! Or a college degree! Or a beautiful spouse! Or that nice new car being advertised! Life would be perfect. Then we get these things.

Yes, life is like that.

It requires our constant attention.

222

Stumbling Toward Enlightenment

Saturday, October 28, 2006

With cooler air comes warmer clothes. And often a quicker pace. As a result of my paralysis, I stumble a lot, especially if I try to go faster, and even worse if holding anything at all, even something like the mail. Over the years I have developed a sort of love/hate relationship with my disability. On the one hand it is a serious pain in the you know what. On the other hand, it is a valuable and ever-present teacher.

Life is like that.

So when I stumble, I mutter something to myself, and depending, it might be addressing that firsthand, or that second hand. In either case, I slow down a bit and place my attention on placing my foot, picking up my foot, and the swing of my arms. I also quickly readjust my thinking.

In many ways I am blessed for living the life I have. I think we all are. Each of us lives. It is our special blessing to appreciate our lives as they are.

223

Freedom

Sunday, October 29, 2006

If you need to believe in something go somewhere else. Zen is not about belief, in fact it is anti-belief. Zen is an experiential thing, call it a practice or a philosophy, or a religion if you will, it is fundamentally an orientation in action.

Beliefs are a hindrance to our experience because, like pillows on our bed, they create a soft comfort zone for our minds to rest. Resting gets us only resting. Moreover, we all too often mistake our "belief" for the thing itself, that thing being an awakened life.

What does it mean then, to live an awakened life?

The cat purrs. The dog runs. I pour coffee. My heart-mind hurts. I love my wife. We make breakfast. Get it?

An awakened life is right in front of your nose.

When we live in the promise or thought of tomorrow, whether it be alive or dead in heaven or Nirvana, we are already in hell. Hell is the striving for something we already possess not being aware that we possess it. So, like the fingers in the Chinese puzzle, relax your grasp and you are free.

224

Appearances

Monday, October 30, 2006

Please accept my apologies for such a late message. Today was a very nice day. The sun was bright and the sky clear. The air was crisp in the morning; warmed in the afternoon, and chilled again this evening. I now sit in my zendo with my pups sleeping nearby. The incense is burning and my small candle is lit. Shortly I will sit down on my zafu and begin my practice.

A reader, Jeff, posted a note on one of my blogs. He cited two postings that seemed to contradict each other:

"If you need to believe in something, go somewhere else. Zen is not about belief, if fact it is anti-belief." - posted by So Daiho Hilbert on Oct 29 2006

"As a religious or philosophical person, we must take our belief, faith, our practices, if they are authentic, out into the world. We must stand for the good against evil. Good and evil are not amorphous concepts. They are practical and political realities." - posted by So Daiho Hilbert on Jun 30 2006

I am deeply flattered by this posting as it clearly suggests Jeff is a serious student who is paying attention to my blatherings. As in all things, Zen or otherwise, two sides of any coin never touch but are deeply connected. I say on one hand, belief is an obstacle, and on the other hand suggest people of principle are believers. I believe wholeheartedly that both are true.

A believer has no need of a light, believing he already possesses the truth. Yet, in truth, only when we turn the light of day toward something does the thing itself become clear.

We must have faith in our practice, in what the Buddha has taught us, and our experience confirms, and at the same time, remain skeptical not only of other people's views, but of our senses and our perceptions, as well. When we look deeply into our own nature and see what is there, there is nothing to fear and nothing to stand against. As Uchiyama-roshi says, we must "open the hand of thought," to which I add, all of life unfolds.

225

Living

Tuesday, October 31, 2006

Mindful living is tiresome. It takes work and exposes us to pain. Most of us cannot live this way and take something. We take a drink, or a hit on a funny looking cigarette, or a cigarette itself. Others, wonder with our bodies, lusting after this delight or that. Some of us hide in our thoughts. Still others fall deeply in love with ourselves and spend hours preening. It all comes to the same thing, increased suffering.

While mindful living takes constant effort and attention, it is the only way to truly appreciate our lives. Exposed to pain? So what else is new, we suffer pain, just as we suffer joy. Wanting one to stay and the other to flee is pointless: they both come and go like waves on the surface of a pond. Change your relationship to the waves, regardless of what we call them, and they disappear as waves.

Takes effort? Of course. Takes attention? Yeppers. So, what else do you have to do with your life but live it?

226

Just Sitting

Wednesday, November 1, 2006

Zazen was good this morning. It is always good to sit still and become yourself. Someone wrote to me and asked what to do in the "sadness phase" of meditation. I am uncertain as to what she meant, but I suspect when she is quiet, sadness emerges from the shadows.

One of the most challenging aspects of zazen is just this. When we sit quietly in stillness, all of our typical distractions are taken away from us. Movement, chewing gum, smoking, drinking, eating, talking, everything is just gone. These things provide cover for the other things that haunt us. So when they are not there, no cover, and bam! There they are, those pesky feelings or thoughts or memories. And we are there to witness them.

OK. So, what's the problem? They are just thoughts, just feelings, just memories. They have no power of their own. They are chimera. It is when we take them and build on them and wish they weren't there or were there more often or whatever that we begin to go crazy.

Zazen is simply about experience. We do not judge the experience. We do not move from it or to it. We just experience. We learn from this experience over time that everything has a life of its own so to speak. Things rise and things fall, just as our breath comes and goes. When we are with the coming and going, no problem; when we resist it, big problem.

As for me, I am just a simple person on a cushion who enjoys being still. Then again, maybe not.

227

Our Teachers

Thursday, November 2, 2006

Through the smallest things in our life do we create ourselves. The way we touch something, the way we treat our friends, strangers, the cashier in the grocery store. Each point of contact with the world around us is a manifestation of our realization. Want to be a buddha, be a Buddha. It is really that simple.

This requires a willingness to be thoughtful and mindful. It also requires a willingness to surrender our ego and to see our Teacher in everything from the highest to the lowest, because in truth, there is no highest, no lowest, and every single thing is buddha.

This is so challenging in a busy world. We feel we must multitask and thus, by definition, live mindlessly on a sort of contemporary autopilot. such a life leads to callous disregard for what is before us. Things, people, animals become means to ends. We do not have the time to see them for the Teachers they are.

I invite each of you to stop. Create a small amount of time in your busy lives to be still. Practice zazen.

228

Zazenkai

Friday, November 3, 2006

Tomorrow we will practice zazen throughout the day. It is Zazenkai day at Zen Center. I look forward to this opportunity to practice with you. If you are not within distance of Zen Center or are otherwise occupied with matters of consequence, please practice mindfulness through your day.

Each day the sun comes up, we are offered the opportunity to become a buddha. Yet these days are numbered. It is up to you not to waste your time.

This means in each act, each breath, of each moment, we are to make ourselves aware of each act, each breath, and each moment. This is attention. It requires practice. When we practice all things change, they come alive. The colors are brighter, the textures are more vibrant, because our senses are keener. We use our attention to open ourselves to the universe.

This is a very good thing.

229

Peaches and Cream; Rocks and Nails

Saturday, November 4, 2006

Today is a good day to spend in meditation. Or in mindfulness. As my finger touches each key, I am aware that each finger is touching a key. I am aware of the muscle movement in my forearm as my fingers extend and contract, aware of the thoughts arising and falling, being recorded on the electronic page of this computer soon to be presented to you.

When we are mindful, we are aware of the things themselves, but also aware that these things come and go. On the one hand we say they are ours, like "my thoughts" but on the other, we notice that thoughts simply are thoughts and they arise and they fall away. A notion of ownership, in a sense, becomes meaningless. In another sense they are quite meaningful, as they originate from our brain, and our brain originates from its connections with all of the other subsystems created by our genetics, even these are connected and originate through interactions with other systems. When we are mindful we are aware that when we eat, we eat ourselves. We touch our partners or a stranger, we touch ourselves. And so we do so with care.

This is a difficult practice and though I try, I often fail at achieving it. The world seems to exist outside of us and can easily crash in bursting this little Buddha Bubble I've just created. Or has it? You know, stress is just another feeling. Loss, love, anger, just feelings. They roll toward us like ocean waves.

Sometimes we resist them, sometimes we embrace them, sometimes we just let go and go with their flow.

Where is it written that everything should be peaches and cream and that we should be as smooth as the cream flowing over the peaches? Aware of the peaches, I am also aware of the rocks and the nails, and the sting of angry, hurtful words.

Our practice is to take this awareness and use it.

230

Being Yourself

Thursday, November 9, 2006

There is a wonderful sun in the sky already here in New Mexico. The sky is clear and it is a nice 66 degrees F. I just returned from morning Zazen. We had a nice turnout for morning, and I made us all pancakes and eggs with coffee. It was really nice sitting at the table together.

We talked about the precepts this morning and I tried to stress that the precepts are not rules. Rules are external, they are brittle, they are decidedly un-Buddhist. The Buddha taught that we are all already completely enlightened beings, meaning that the precepts are actually fluid doorways to a true expression of our Buddha nature. When we drop away the clutter and see directly with a clear mind, there is no separation between us and the precepts. We are the precepts.

Today, please be the Buddha you are.

231

Vote!

Friday, November 10, 2006

Today is the day for us in the United States to decide as a group who will represent us. It is very important that you participate in this election. As we have seen, elections are often won or lost on the basis of voters choosing to come or not come to the polls.

While I cannot endorse a candidate or a party, I can ask you to vote in a way that clearly reflects our values as followers of the Buddha Way. So, in the voting booth, vote as the buddha you are.

232

On Being and Becoming, Sorta

Saturday, November 11, 2006

Most of the time we are not buddhas, but rather, buddha wannabees. We buzz around with our nice thoughts and wonderful words strung together ever so easily, like colored beads on a string. And then we wash the dishes, watch television, and have a life with our spouses and children.

At Zen Center, we can be the buddhas we think we are, but at home, the clothes come off and a whole other person arises. Is this so?

If we are pretending to be something we imagine to be "Buddhist" then we are not buddhas. On the other hand, if we are annoyed or angry or afraid or lonely, this does not mean we are not "Buddhist" either, and if we are genuinely these things, aware that we are these things, then, in fact we are buddhas.

Buddhas are nothing if not authentic in the moment.

Last night I had occasion to feel tremendous hurt, anger, sorrow, humiliation, and compassion, in that order. We attended a service at the synagogue after having supported a local poet at a reading at a local bookstore and having just returned from the mountains. A small group in attendance. None of the people we typically attend with were there. A long time Temple member was leading the service as the rabbi is on sabbatical. This person used the d'var Torah (sermon time) to comment on hospitality. Good. But then she brought up the divisions in the congregation, the rancor at the annual meeting from months ago, and essentially chastised those "new members" who caused such a hurtful stir. My wife and I were two of those members.

So, I sat in the synagogue and heard what she had to say. I decided that rather than react to my hurt, I should open myself as much as I could to her and her point of view. She was hurt by the conflict in the synagogue and hurt creates a kind of personal fundamentalism, as Pema Chodron beautifully pointed out. When we are hurt, we close ourselves and begin immediately to mount a counterattack to stop the hurt. We blame the person hurting us for our pain.

What this does is close us off even further and we no longer hear the person, nor do we want to. Instead, we either want to fight or flee.

Since getting up and leaving in the middle of a person's talk would be rude and very disrespectful, fleeing was not an option.

This offered me an opportunity to practice. And I witnessed my body tense, my reptilian mind emerge, and duck for cover as I swatted it away with my beads which were getting pretty warm in my fingers. I saw and felt her hurt, her anger, and her sense of righteousness. I saw that it was necessary for her to do this. I hope it helped her. I felt great compassion for his often-brittle woman who uses her intelligence and vitriol to defend herself.

We came home directly, My Little Honey did not want to stay for the Oneg (a joyous snack party after the service) for fear she would "say" something. It was just as well. In the car I drove in silence and processed much of my feelings. At home I entered my zendo, lit a stick of incense and sat on my cushion until it was ash.

233

Open Societies

Sunday, November 12, 2006

Mt alarm clock, in the form of furry friend, Tripper's tongue, woke me at 5:30 this morning. What does a dog know about weekends? So, I got up and made the coffee. Opened the laptop and began to read the morning mail.

A couple of messages from someone who thought I expelled them from my group went off on me. I had no idea what she was talking about. I wrote her back asking her to explain herself. Some other messages from friends who were concerned about the issues I brought up in yesterday's note. I am sitting with those. And a lot of support for sharing my feelings. It is apparently very important that people who are perceived to be religious leaders be real and open with their experience. I believe this is true.

As a therapist, I was struck by the work of a psychologist who wrote a book called the Transparent Self. In this work, he talked about the notion that self-disclosure was essential at getting to the truth in an interview with a patient. Now, to some extent, our society has been riding on the self-disclosure wagon and everyone seems to be playing a game of king on the mountain as regards war stories. But this is not genuine self-disclosure.

Being open means being willing to receive as well as give. To receive, one must be willing to set aside self and really listen to another. This means listening without processing an answer. It means self-disclosing for the sake of intimacy and closeness and thus is done judiciously and with purpose.

In Zen we self-disclose to acknowledge our realization of deep interconnectedness with each other. We learn that we are all one in the same beings, buddhas seeking to crack out of the shell of delusion. The light that shines forth from the disclosures of our struggles can be heart-warming.

The sharing of self in public or private is directly related in my opinion to the nature of the organization. The more rigid the organization and tighter the hierarchy, the less public disclosure and the more private disclosure (in the form of quiet gossip). The less rigid and more open the organization the higher the level of public disclosure and thus the more open the rancor. In very orthodox institutions there are very strict rules for deportment. Thus, our need to disclose is forced underground so to speak. Restricted to small circles, gossip spends its time with coffee spoons. In more liberal and open institutions, roles and rules are more relaxed, everyone is seen as having validity and a voice and, well, there you have it: a room full of experts!

We hope in liberal settings that people will behave themselves. Most of the time they do. Frankly, I vote for open societies regardless, but it does mean we must learn how to be human together.

234

No Chicken Little Here!

Monday, November 13, 2006

The sounds of early morning are delightfully few and far between. Stillness. After the dogs go out, they curl up to nap. I sip my coffee and read the morning news. It seems the world always appears to be falling apart. I close that screen and open another.

Our world, in spite of everything, is not falling apart. People care deeply for one another. For every act of violence, there are countless people there to care for those injured. For every disaster, human beings come together to pick up the pieces and rebuild. Billions of us live together, most with scarce resources, and yet each day we demonstrate our true nature as compassionate beings. In truth, the news stories, the pictures of death and destruction, these are the oddities. We must keep that in mind.

As we go through our day today, let's keep our hearts open. Embracing the world is a wonderful way to embrace yourself.

235

The Senses

Tuesday, November 14, 2006

There are some sounds that are very comforting. The sound I hear right now is Pepper's breath as he sleeps by my feet. The sound yesterday was the laughter of good friends enjoying a serendipitous meal together. Sounds are a true picture of the nature of things, we cannot hold onto them. And memory is pale in comparison. Yet there they are in our experience. Direct, they lift us up yet leave us just instantly.

All of the senses are like this.

We suffer when we try to keep them close. We suffer when we value one over another.

So, regardless of the sound, hear it; regardless of the sight, see it. Appreciate the moment.

236

Being Real

Friday, November 17, 2006

This past Wednesday evening we had one of our Zen Center members who lives in El Paso arrive with his daughter. She is a delightful young lady, smart as a whip, and just a joy to practice with. I invited her to be my assistant and ring the small bell at the appropriate times during the evening. We say together and then we studied a story of the Buddha together. She served our tea before the Dharma talk.

Having children at the Zen Center is a real delight. Children bring a very special energy, as well as a wonderful perspective, to our practice. I have found that children are often very interested in being present, perhaps because they live their lives that way. We can reinforce this and learn from it ourselves by being in the presence of These great teachers.

But first we need to get off our adult high horse.

How? Zazen teaches us that all things are our teachers when our self drops away. Being willing to drop away our self-importance goes hand in hand. Books such as "The Little Prince" and "The Velveteen Rabbit" are really bodhisattvas who lead us to important realizations.

237

On Being Outside the Box

Saturday, November 18, 2006

Is there ever a time when we are ready to live as completely as possible? It would seem we are often living with one foot in the grave, "Oh, don't do that, you'll get hurt!" "Oh, that is just too risky, better not go there!" And so on.

I don't know. I wonder about this sometimes.

One of the reasons we don't live to our full potential is fear, but not so much of getting hurt in the ordinary sense. Rather, this is fear of a different sort; getting hurt in the psychic sense. We are afraid of what people will think of us if we are just ourselves. So we put on, we dress the part, and play roles, never allowing our true selves to emerge.

I remember how liberating it was to find out that even if I make a complete fool of myself, if done honestly, it really didn't matter. People can be hurtful, true. But mostly they are very compassionate and caring human beings. Such liberation is compelling. And I believe people respond best to authentic human beings.

I sometimes laugh a lot. I am also sometimes depressed. I enjoy being with people most of the time. Negative energy and people who seem to be dying before their time are a challenge for me. When I am in their presence, I feel the drain. Yet, I think this is a key practice. To learn to be present in each and every moment and to be open to every being regardless of how I might be feeling at that moment. How else can one be of service? We really don't have the luxury of picking and choosing our moments to be buddhas

Each of us is a universal being. We each share Original Mind. Each of us is a particular being. Each of us possess unique qualities. It is up to us to discover and value these things. Being a real person is a necessary first step.

238

Tangles

Sunday, November 19, 2006

"Not the faults of others, nor what others have done or left undone, but one's own deeds, done and left undone, should one consider." the Buddha

The truth is so hard to take sometimes. We live in a world where it seems we are always judging. Well, I should really speak for myself. I live in a world where I seem to always be judging. In this world is pain and suffering and I realize I am its cause.

If I were to place my sole attention on being the person I know I am, no problem. If I were to look at others as myself, no problem...well, maybe big problem, since I can be pretty hard on myself. But you get the point.

It is so important to take care of one's own business, it is a first step to being upright. Yet so much easier to look somewhere else and pay attention to others.

When we sit zazen we are left with only ourselves. Just us with our breath and our mind and our senses. Yikes! Still, if we have the courage to continue to sit there, we begin to see clearly the work that needs to be done. The ball of yarn begins to unravel of its own accord and there we are, free of the tangles of delusion.

So, we get up off the cushion and do what is there for us to do. All the while letting others do the same.

239

Matsuoka

Tuesday, November 21, 2006

Today is a very special day. We honor Matsuoka-roshi today. For those of you who do not know, Rev. Dr. Soyu Matsuoka-roshi is my Dharma grandfather. He established several Zen Centers in the US in the sixties, seventies, and eighties. Atlanta, Chicago, Long Beach, and through my Teacher, Las Cruces and Cloudcroft. Little is known about him, as he never published a book (although there is one in process). He was born and died in the same month, November.

Without his effort, courage, and willingness to come to America from Sojiji, we would not be gathered here together in person or online. Nine bows to him.

240

Off an Afternoon

Saturday, November 25, 2006

This morning was a wonder. Tate woke with a serious hunger! Screeching until he had breakfast. The Zoo was too much for him, I guess, and he went to sleep last night hard and fast. At the Zoo earlier in the day, I had walked enough and sat down near the Pandas to finish reading a book I thoughtfully tucked in my shirt.

It was a wonderful experience to sit and witness the families, the excitement of the children, and the sounds of wildlife. Pema Chodron's book on peace in times of war is a very good effort at teaching us to be present in the face of danger. I closed it and sat on the forward edge of my seat outside under some trees.

A man noticed me sitting there and asked if I were meditating. I smiled and said, "I am." He replied that he was "Chillin'" as well, as he sorted the chairs and otherwise cleaned the area. He was Black and a hard worker; I am White and hardly work at all. He had a heavy gold cross around his neck, I had a string of 108 beads running through my fingers. He was Zen in motion, I was Zen in stillness, we both shared the moment together.

Life is like that.

241

Knowing what we know?

Sunday, November 26, 2006

When we practice zazen, we are just present with ourselves. Self encounters self. Sometimes we argue with each other, sometimes we run from each other, sometimes we watch movies of one, none of this is zazen. But every time we notice that we are doing these things and bring ourselves back to the present moment, we are practicing zazen. Zazen is in the noticing. It is the being, not the becoming.

When we encounter something and act like a human being we ask questions, sometimes out loud and directly, but more often secretly and to ourselves. What's this? Who is this? Where is this? Why is this? And we put these things into a timeline of 'when is this?' All perfectly natural. But all in the mind. Each of these questions take us far away from the experience of the thing we are encountering.

We answer our questions and believe we know something about the thing when in fact we know something about our thoughts about the thing. And there is a dramatic difference. This is why we can say it is a mistake to say, incense becomes ash.

So, the next time you experience something new. Stop at the point of experience. Keep the experience and let the thoughts about it go. This is zazen.

242

The Refuges

Tuesday, November 28, 2006

There were two of us at Zen Center this morning. Michelle and I sat a solid period of zazen, I made pancakes, we ate, then sipped a morning cup of coffee and talked about the Three Refuges. These are the Buddha, the Dharma, and the Sangha.

It might surprise you to know these are not always what you think they are. The Buddha is not the person of the Buddha, nor the statue of the Buddha, nor an idea of the Buddha. The Buddha is just being awake. Seeing without distortion, like a mountain in crisp morning air. So, we take refuge in being awake. The Dharma is the teaching, but not really. The Teaching is not the Dharma. Once uttered it is stale. The Dharma is reality just as it is, unvarnished, sweet or stinky, smacking us upside our head. When we see clearly, with open eyes, no preconception, and experience this, this is Dharma. It is the truth of our lives. Sangha is the world that supports us and our practice.

So, forget stone Buddhas, fancy scriptures, and pretty temples. These are not our home. Our home is in our breath just now. Now. Now. Now.

Buddhas and sutras and priests can be hindrances if we see them as something to emulate. These are just pictures of the thing. Be the thing itself. How?

Right now, let your eyes close halfway, release your breath, and be present.

How hard is that?

243

Be a Light

Wednesday, November 29, 2006

A friend writes that I rarely quote sutras in my messages. He also points out that I rarely reply to comments. There is truth in this sorta. If we understand sutras as scripture, he is correct. Scripture is what it is, a finger pointing to something. The danger of scripture study is that we can get to a point where we value the scripture more than what it is pointing to. And what exactly is that? Every scripture is about practice, that is to say, some aspect of living out an awakened life.

Sutra study aids us. It is a corrective lesson. It helps us sit upright, so to speak, but it is not the sitting itself. Sitting we must do. Life must be lived and when lived with open eyes the buddha is realized.

Often my morning messages are replies. Your messages suggest topics. I clarify - or attempt to clarify - with my messages. I write two of these a day. One I post to you on these lists and the other to my blog at Yahoo 360. I try to keep up with the direct correspondence as much as possible, yet life must be lived. Puppies need to be walked, Zen Center needs to be taken care of, and Little Honeys listened to and engaged with. Life is like that.

The lessons of life are our own. They are right there in the lives we live. We only need to turn the lamp on them to realize them, as the Buddha himself said in his Parinirvana sutra. I will leave you this morning with that: be a light unto yourself.

244

Stepping Out

November 30, 2006

This morning my wrist alarm surprised me. I pushed back the down comforter and was greeted with a chill in the air. We have two alternatives, pull the comforters back up or throw them off and step out into the cool morning air. Our lives, every moment of our lives, is just like that.

We can pull the covers over us and stay warm and comfortable in what we know or we can cast off what we know and enter life with open eyes.

This choice comes to us a million times a day. It is the choice between being automatic and genuine. The choice between patience and impatient, generous or greedy, wise or shallow. The "right" choice is always both the more challenging and the more rewarding.

Yet we should not make this choice on that basis. Rather, we chose it because we are buddhas being buddhas.

245

Living and Learning

Monday, December 4, 2006

Our Rohatsu sesshin was a powerful one. We were completely full and on Sunday, had several people sitting in the kitchen and two in the foyer of the Zen Center. Soon we will need a larger building, I suppose.

A deep bow of gratitude to each of you in attendance!

We all sat zazen very well. I must say, though, that our silence was broken late Saturday afternoon when one of the participants, Jeremy, requested the kyosaku and as I went to smack his shoulder I missed, hitting his neck! As I bowed and apologized, the whole Sangha erupted in laughter...this is what sitting hour after hour will do to you!

Sesshin should not be tense. Neither should zazen. Neither should life. These are experience. Experience itself is neutral. It is what it is. We add to it our various spins. We like this, we dislike that. People should be this way, not that way. And so on. It is this discerning mind that takes us away from Buddha Mind.

Buddha Mind appreciates life as it is: sweet, sour, salty, torrid. Each of these is a pointer, so to speak. Appreciate and use the pointer, but then move on. So, while we can laugh at the Roshi's mistake, we should not carry it with us. I need to be completely mindful and present with my kyosaku and not assume I know how to use it well.

What do you need?

246

What's Your Moment?

Tuesday, December 5, 2006

This morning is different. I was up late last night and fell asleep in the Zendo. My Little Honey slept in the bedroom. My dogs slept in the Zendo with me, as did Pete-kitty. So this morning My Little Honey crawled onto the futon and found a place amid all the little heart beats. Of course, Tripper was very unhappy that he had a rival for my attention. Rather than unfolding, this folded into an awakening experience for me: all hair and wet tongues and heartbeats.

So, I got up and made the coffee, decided I had enough enlightenment and sat down in the living room to clear my head of the fur and hair that can be my life.

Since the coffee is made, My Little Honey has decided she should join me, and all the other heartbeats followed. It is said that wherever we go, there we are.

Life is like that.

No escape.

So, what can we do? We enjoy the moment by shifting gears, as is said today. We let go of our expectations and enjoy the ride as it is. When we consciously do this it is possible to be taught. Drivers never learn, they are too busy driving.

You might say, but how do we ever get anywhere? And I answer, where is there to get? When we achieve something we want something else. We have something, it gets old and we want something new. When we have some money, we want some more. When there is always somewhere to go, we never arrive.

Yet, to live in the moment does not mean there is no tomorrow or that we cannot plan for, and build toward, a future. It means that in each moment, even if it is a planning moment, we experience it as fully and as completely as possible. To do this requires something of us.

We have to disappear and allow the present to be us.

247

Appreciate

Wednesday, December 6, 2006

We talk a lot about being present. Yet thoughts of pleasant things take us away as well. Thoughts of quiet beaches or retreats in the mountains or just a walk along a river at dusk. One wonders what it is that is so challenging about this very moment in our lives.

Perhaps we do not know how to appreciate what we have and perhaps we are led to believe by advertisers that what we have is never enough. Our culture is a consumer culture, sadly. Because consumers eat their surroundings rather than participate in them. Surroundings are for our pleasure, our toys are for our amusement, people are to meet our needs: we are the center of the universe.

Being present means being a full participant in life as it is.

My Little Honey has a wonderful habit of finding the value in whatever she has and in whatever she is doing. She has some old yarn, she makes something with it. Everything has its value and she finds real pleasure in each thing. She can giggle at the silliest things. I hear her and look over, and there she is admiring an old piece of cloth, part of a doll, or some little thing she has just knitted...that is to say, created with her own hands.

These are moments of real value. The pictures on the t.v. are just phosphorescent dots on a screen.

248

Our Own Authority

Thursday, December 7, 2006

Someone wrote to ask me to speak more on the notion of walking in one's own authority. Since today is December 7th, the day Japan attacked Pearl Harbor, perhaps this is a good day for such a comment. Brian Victoria wrote a book entitled Zen at War and in it he reveals the behavior of Japanese Zen monks during World War II. Apparently, many were fervent nationalists, anti-Semites, and other such very un-Buddhist things. The question arises, then, how could this be?

First, a monk's vows do not exempt a monk from his or her civic obligations. We should all be good citizens. The question is, what does that mean? My sense is that a good citizen is a buddha. This means a person whose eyes are wide open, who lives in non-dualist terms and can easily move in the relative and absolutes that make our universe.

Walking in one's own authority requires inside information, so to speak. This inside information is a realization of our true nature, our original face, if you will: that face "we" had before "our" parents were born. Such information is always with us, it is a part of us, but we must find it ourselves through our practice.

We could call this face God, if you will, or Buddha Mind, or the Universal, or simply Vast Emptiness. It really doesn't matter what it is called, what matters is that it is both experienced and actualized by us in our lives. When this happens, the precepts become our own manifestations of this realization so that when we are in particular social situations, we know what to do and this doing is our own, as well. Yet it corresponds precisely and exactly to Buddha Dharma.

This is outside meeting inside and vice-versa: resolving both.

So, when a monk is asked to do something which goes against his or her Buddha nature, he or she must find a skillful way of engaging the request to turn it into a teaching lesson for the universe. This is what it means to "save all beings." The lessons can be myriad.

This said, it is possible, probable even, that religious institutions become corrupt and power-hungry. In Zen, this is also the case. Monks argue over status and Temple politics, shuffling for this advantage or that: the same as any work environment. They can also become servants of the civil government and the mob majority. However, it should not be. If we work the program as is said in other paths, then "letting go of self" and humility are the greatest teachers. So there's the rub, when letting go of self, where does our authority go?

A buddha understands that our authority is never ours but is an aspect of our True Nature. One who has realized this True Nature manifests it; one who has not, who only aspires to do so, does not. Seeking this authority in a religious structure will never do. In fact, the religious structure becomes a serious hindrance to achieving Clear Mind.

Monks who do bad things are not walking in their own authority and this is their most serious sin.

249

Our Morning Star

Friday, December 8, 2006

Yes, the earth has clearly tilted. Cooler temps, snow in places, and a cloudy sky this morning. We hustle just a little more in the morning and wrap ourselves with layers of clothing. I try not to give in so much to this temptation. Cold can be refreshing. Just as heat can be soothing. Yet too much of either and we are in trouble.

Today we should recognize the Buddha's achievement. He worked so hard for so many years only to discover in an instant that what he sought he already possessed, as do all of us. The most profound teaching, I suspect, is to stop seeking. This stopping, this deep abiding in silence with self allows for our release of self, paradoxically, and the concomitant discovery that there is no abiding self.

Let us each witness the morning star in the same way.

250

The Silence of the Lion

Saturday, December 9, 2006

The day is unfolding slowly, as Saturdays do. There are clouds in the sky and the air is cool. I am parked under a down comforter with Tripper at my side. My Little Honey is talking to our daughter and getting ready to leave for Knitters Guild. I will be alone with the furboys for the morning.

Whatever will I do?

Setting aside the obvious dog walking, breakfast eating, meditation, and writing, nothing special. This is as it should be. Life lived as one page to the next where our focus is on the page we are reading is best. Other pages are what they are and will turn as they may, but this very page is us.

> *Pete-kitty sits*
> *like a small lion*
> *staring at my fingers*
> *as they press these keys.*
> *Silence unfolds.*

251

Where's the Beef?

Sunday, December 10, 2006

As we awaken we say, "This morning I vow with all beings to see the world clearly as it is and to end violence and bring compassion to all beings." In the evening we say, "This evening, as I go to sleep, may all beings rest and be renewed through peace and love."

In this way we open and close our day by placing our attention on our true purpose in life, to nurture and support all beings. It is not that we are instruments of these things, rather, we are these things. Being the instrument of something creates a separation between the thing and the tool, as if they were not exactly the same. Being an instrument of compassion is not the same as being compassion.

We each have work to do through each day for the rest of our lives. The paycheck of this work is immediate. When we open our eyes, there it is. Both work and reward are the exact same thing: a manifestation of our true nature.

252

Careful

Monday, December 11, 2006

In Zen we practice to see our True Nature. Be careful!

Our True Nature
is the Universe
and the Universe
has nothing
to stand upon.

So, what happens when we confront our Self? See our impermanence, our absolute emptiness? Maybe we say "Eureka!" I think not.

Most ordinary human beings, those Dogen calls mortals, require something to stand on. they require a reference point, something to define themselves against: like form and space in a painting. But with our True Nature, we see these are ever in motion, nothing substantial, everything like the clouds in the sky.

Seeing our True Nature, we step into the world of the Buddhas: immortal where each breath is a manifest opportunity, each touch, the creation of kindness and compassion, each step a walk into infinity.

253

Foundation

Tuesday, December 12, 2006

Those here seeking wisdom and knowledge are welcome, however, it is important to orient yourself to how this process is understood in Zen Buddhism. Wisdom and knowledge are often thought to be something that exist outside of us, that can be imparted by one person to another. That is a dualistic notion and is incorrect.

Wisdom and knowledge are innate: we all possess them. We practice to see what is already there within us and before us. We practice to eliminate the proscenium that separates the actor from the universe.

So, if you are seeking something from me or others, stop. Seek it from yourself. How? Create a time each day to practice zazen. Practicing zazen regularly is a gate to understanding and realization. Let nothing get in the way of this regular practice. It becomes your spiritual foundation, literally.

Then post your experience. Posting is a process of self-examination and awareness. I ask that replies be explorations rather than fingers pointing to supposed errors.

254

Forgiveness

Wednesday, December 13, 2006

A friend asked me about forgiveness. I thought it would be nice to say a few things about it. Yet this thing we call forgiveness is very tricky as it points to the fact that we, ourselves, are holding on to some pain inflicted on us by another. This causes us to suffer. Sometimes the person we wish to forgive hasn't a clue that he has hurt us in the first place.

So, at first blush, we might think that forgiveness is about absolving someone else and letting them off the hook, in truth it is we who are hooked by our anger and hurt. This is one of those curious little scenarios in life that can actually demonstrate to us just how deeply interconnected (and often clueless) we are.

It is that very interconnectedness that makes forgiveness truly possible. And our cluelessness that makes it possible for us to suffer for so long. When we think of how another person hurt us, then look inside and see how we are being just as hurtful against ourselves, we can see our humanity. Each glimpse into our human condition provides us an opportunity to learn. ..and change, or rather, transform.

The first step in forgiveness, then, is to forgive ourselves for carrying such pain and hurt with us for so long. We may not be ready to do this. The pain of an experience may be very important to us. Sometimes this pain is a marker of our prior state, say our innocence, then we are victimized and our pain recalls not only the victimization, but our state prior to our victimization, as well. We blame the perpetrator for both our victimization and the loss of our identity as an ordinary person. Who really wants to confront change so directly?

So, we desperately hold on to what we thought we were, knowing we are not, and feel great anger toward the person who made all this happen. It is now we who are victimizing ourselves.

When we have had enough of this, we will stop. We stop when we discover that we have worth beyond an experience somewhere in the past. We stop when we realize our present is our choice and our responsibility. We stop when we realize it does no good to continue holding on.

This is a liberating moment.

255

Our Hurt

Thursday, December 14, 2006

So many of you have written to ask how we can forgive and move on! It makes me think that perhaps we are taking ourselves way too seriously. People are people, we each seem to live in our own world made of our own thought and feelings, yet we somehow expect others to not only understand us, but perceive within our worldview. This is like asking two hurt puppies to nurture each other.

Will addressing the person who has hurt us make it better? Sometimes. It is doubtful. Only if we possess extraordinary listening skills would this be advised, in my opinion. Getting something "off our chest" is too often for our benefit, yet we go around rationalizing that it is for the benefit of the other. In fact, it actually amounts to 'dumping' our load on someone else's shoulders.

If someone has hurt us, perhaps we should look deeply into the hurt. Often hurt is more about our expectation of another's behavior than anything else. We expect a sister-in-law to behave a certain way, or a boyfriend or a girlfriend to love us in a way we believe they should, but then they behave in a way we either don't understand or cannot accept. We see this as an affront to ourselves, sometimes to our values, but most often to our expectations for their behavior.

Ooops, there goes that self-righteous ball a-rolling!

What to do? The hardest work of all: nothing. Sit still and let the universe take care of itself. Hurt only remains with us if we keep picking at it. A daily practice of zazen along with on-going mindfulness practice can be of great benefit with this.

This is very hard work. It requires something of us: that we sit on our hands (to use an old chess training method) and not snap off moves so quickly. Easy? Hardly. I have been at this a very long time and I still knee-jerk with my mouth on far too many occasions. Still, I am aware immediately as I am doing this. And in that awareness is often the desire to be still and not react. Our practice makes it possible to be present without being so swept away by the floods of feelings and thoughts. And on those increasingly rare times when we are swept away by our anger or hurt, we are able to pull ourselves out more quickly, on the one hand, and experience the suffering we have caused, on the other. These then become opportunities for personal and social growth.

Now, to take my own advice.

256

Daily Message

Friday, December 15, 2006

One way that Zen differentiates itself from other religions, even from Buddhism itself, is on the issue of belief. Zen Buddhists are nothing if not iconoclastic. (An iconoclast is a breaker of icons). There is a famous saying, "If you meet the Buddha on the road, kill him!" While this should not be taken literally, it should be held closely.

Buddhas, images of Buddhas, stories of Buddhas, miracles of Buddhas are all fictions. We create these images and stories and then use them as yardsticks against which we measure ourselves. This is wrong-headed.

When we break the images, burn the stories, and tear up the scriptures, we are on our own and must confront ourselves. This is the heart of Buddhist practice, and it is not for everyone.

We sit facing a wall. Our bodies upright, our eyes open, our attention on everything present. No belief. No doctrine. No dogma. Just this.

So, this morning at the Zendo, I lit a stick of incense, bowed and sat down on my cushion. Facing the wall, I met myself. Facing myself, I let myself fall away. What is left? Buddha.

257

Making Light

Saturday, December 16, 2006

Last night was so delightful. We went to the synagogue for Friday evening services which was a children's service and Hanukkah candle lighting. We had a dozen or so menorahs on a table and before we ate the children recited the blessings over and over as they themselves lit the first night's candles. Such traditions are as important as they are beautiful.

This season is a time of light. Menorahs, Christmas trees, and in the Buddhist tradition, the light of the Buddha's Enlightenment itself.

To bring light into the world is an act of creation. It is not hope, faith, or charity. It is the thing itself. It is dark, we make light. We light a candle, we turn a switch, we dress a tree, but as human beings we make light by cracking out of our shells and unfolding ourselves to the universe.

From a Zen Buddhist perspective, light and dark are literally of our own creation. We do good or we do bad, and these things are judged more from our intent than from the outcome. If you are a theist, and you must have a God in your lives, you can easily understand this as God working through you. You and God are partners in creation: you are His hands, His eyes, His fingers, but you are also His mind...and He is yours. In Zen, we see this as "Big Mind."

This is the open expanse of time and space, light and dark, the breath before the breath, of life and death. Now, go make light.

258

Time

Sunday, December 17, 2006

My goodness here it is Sunday once more. Have you noticed how time is so relative to age? When we are young and imagine all the benefits of being older, we look so forward to the passing of time that it slows. And as aging people, we are not so looking forward to the end of days, and time just becomes a torrent!

Life is like that.

The lesson is to not seek, but to be present. The relativity of time is teaching us this lesson and when we are ready to receive the teaching it is very good news.

Being present is timeless. Being present is being as it is. Our discriminating mind, doing what it does, takes us away from this and thrusts us into the relativity of judgment, recrimination, and expectation. This mind must be mastered, but to master it is not to control it, it is to passively witness it.

Going back to an image I frequently use: the motor is racing, but you don't have to put the car in gear. Let it race. And as it races, you are serenely reflecting on its racing. Hoping it will stop racing will slow time down.

259

Mountains and Rivers in Morning

Monday, December 18, 2006

The silence of the early morning is broken by a siren in the distance. Like a bell, it brings me back to myself as I sit here to write to you.

Morning is not delicate. Open space, it receives sound and light. When through the day, such sound and light is everywhere, morning is still morning. Morning, an equivalent of zazen, does not require silence.

Just as a mountain sits as the rain pounds it, the people trample on it, or fire burns it, so morning opens to the day. Mountain does not require separateness. Morning and mountain are the same as zazen.

The river flows through the valley and as it flows it does not care whether a tree falls in it. It embraces the tree. Eventually the tree and the river become one. The river does not require a path. Morning, mountain and river are the same as zazen.

Sometimes it is our view of a thing that blinds us to seeing it.

260

Faith, Belief and Practice

Wednesday, December 20, 2006

Practice of the Buddha's Way requires our diligence and constant attention. In fact, these are the Buddha Way. In the morning, we open our eyes and consider the universe with compassion. We embrace our lives and embrace each other. This is our life.

One does not believe in Buddha. One does not believe in Dharma. One does not believe in Sangha. There is no dogma, no doctrine, no belief at all. There is just the practice of noticing, the practice of loving, and the practice of embracing.

In all of this, the core practice is faith: not in a God or a set of beliefs, but in ourselves and the universe. Such faith enables us to trust silence. It enables us to trust others. It is these that are the most challenging aspects of our practice.

261

The Life of Buddha

Thursday, December 21, 2006

Last night at Zen Center we held a "Movie Night." A Sangha member, Joshua, brought in a DVD projector. We sat on our zafus against one in the Zendo and projected the film on the other. I had brought in bags of party mix and some soft drinks. We had a very nice evening together.

The film was "the Life of the Buddha." It was a French made film, circa 2003, a documentary in English, and was beautifully photographed. It was essentially an anthropological and sociological study of the Buddha's life. The filmmakers interviewed countless Indians on location in India, and followed the archaeological investigations into the Buddha's life. Religious teachers from various traditions told the stories of the Buddha's birth, training, seeking, enlightenment, teaching, and death. These provided the necessary thread through the film.

In the end, however, after all is said and done, we should know that even such a one as the Buddha, was just a man and all that we say about him is fantasy. The real Buddha is the Universe aware of Itself in and through us.

When we make an idol of the Buddha and forget he was just a man, we do him and ourselves a grave disservice. What the Buddha taught is that we should turn our light inward, we should not be deceived by the icons and religions and philosophies and glitter that surrounds us, but rather we should unfold ourselves as universal witness.

In this way become Buddha.

262

On Being Alone

Friday, December 22, 2006

Another Friday. Hmmm. For those of you about to leave for work and those already at work, please enjoy your day today. Remember each moment is what it is; it is we who add the good or bad of it.

Last night before bed, I was studying a short sutra on being alone. The Buddha was teaching in this scripture that literally being alone was not necessary, nor was it a particularly good practice as seeking this way places our attention on the "I" of the equation.

There are some who prefer to be alone. I was one of them. I rationalized this by romanticizing the thing, you know, mental pictures of a seeker away from the crowd, treading the road less traveled, and so on. Yet, this was a form of delusion. It is a trap just as wickedly poisonous as that of seeking a crowd for approval. The truth is, I was uncomfortable with people, insecure in myself I relied far too heavily on their opinions of me for my opinion of myself.

The Buddha taught that the best way to be alone was to be mindful wherever we are. This way of mindfulness means, essentially, to practice being "all one." When we live as all one, our literal singularity is the universe, and we are its sense organs.

Practice to be a partner in the process.

263

Peace

Sunday, December 31, 2006

This morning, way before sunrise, I woke to go to a local church as I was invited to participate in an International Prayer for Peace. The air was chilly, 28 degrees. The church had a fairly large number of people there for a 5:00 AM service.

I dropped my cushion on the floor at the back, bowed, and took my seat. Only the minister saw me enter. I enjoyed my small anonymity and listened to the various prayers as they were recited one after another: Muslim, Hindu, Jewish, Jain, Christian, Nichiren Buddhist, even a Native American prayer. I was asked to close the service with a few remarks.

The prayers were beautiful. Most beseech God for peace and asked for a world of compassion and understanding. So much desire for peace in that room. I could feel the people's need for serenity; it was almost palpable.

In between each prayer a bell was invited to ring.

I sat with complete attention.

When it came time for me to speak, I felt myself get up off my cushion and walk easily to the podium. I placed my attention on my breath, looked out at the group, and began to speak.

Peace, I said, was not something we should seek. Peace is something we are. We are peace when we set aside ourselves and our desires, our ego and our craving. We are peace when we open ourselves to others and listen to them as they speak. This is the work of peacemaking. It is deeply challenging, but very rewarding work.

This year I vow to not need to be in charge of anything. This year I vow to share. This year I vow to listen as deeply as I am capable to those addressing me. This year I vow to accept all beings as they are, warts and all. This year I vow to replace anger with love, hurt with compassion, and intolerance with patience. This is how peace happens. I know that I will not always be successful, but I vow to forgive myself when not and continue on with this work. If nothing else, I believe we are all worth the effort.

NOTES